THE NECESSARY STEPS TO GLORY

No eye saw, nor ear heard, nor the heart of man conceived, what God has prepared for those who love Him.
1 Corinthians 2:9

WHAT STEP ARE YOU ON?

- Glorification
- Maturity
- Sanctification
- Sanctifying Faith
- Regeneration
- Justification
- Saving Faith
- Confession
- Repentance
- Conviction
- Lost

The Necessary Steps to Glory

Requests for information should be addressed to:
Evangel Publishing House
2000 Evangel Way
P.O. Box 189
Nappanee, Indiana 46550
Phone: (800) 253-9315
Internet: www.evangelpublishing.com

All biblical quotes are from the King James version.

All rights reserved. No part of this publication may be reproduced, stored in a retrieval system, or transmitted in any form or by any means–electronic, mechanical, photocopy, recording, or any other–except for brief quotations in printed reviews, without the prior permission of Evangel Publishing House, P.O. Box 189, Nappanee, Indiana 46550.

Cover Design by Matthew Gable

ISBN: 1-928915-80-9
Library of Congress Catalog Card Number: 2006900310
Printed by Evangel Press, Nappanee, IN
Printed in the United States of America

5 6 7 8 9 EP 8 7 6 5 4 3 2 1

TABLE OF CONTENTS

Preface vii
"In the beginning God" ix

1. Lost Man 1
   Why is he lost? What is the proof?

2. Conviction 31
   What is conviction and why is it necessary?

3. Repentance 41
   What does repentance mean as the corner stone of our Faith?

4. Confession is not forgiveness 51
   When is confession genuine?

5. Saving Faith 57
   What is the difference between Saving Faith and Faith?

6. Justification 71
   What does it mean to be justified?

7. Regeneration 85
   When does this walk start and what does it reveal?

8. Sanctifying Faith 99
   Why sanctifying faith?

9. Sanctification 109
   What is sanctification and why is this necessary?

10. Maturity 149
    What is maturity and its importance?

11. Glorification 165
    The ultimate

This work is dedicated to my dear companion of 54 years who has already traveled these steps and even now, is experiencing the ultimate in sitting at the Master's table.

PREFACE

This manuscript has come about by absolute necessity for teaching my laymen. I was not in the ministry long until it was evident that my people did not know what they believed, nor why they believed what they did believe. Furthermore, they did not know where they were in their present Spiritual lives. This was not only true in my church, but as I began traveling from church to church, the same situation appeared continually.

The purpose is to give good people a sense of direction to find their way through all kinds of church vanity and Spiritual lukewarmness. Their confusion deepens by not understanding Scriptural doctrines, and just where they are in their every day Christian walk. The enemy delights in this kind of Spiritual chaos. At times, the uncertainty becomes unbearable and ends up in utter bewilderment and often Spiritual defeat. There is no Spiritual victory in this type of inner perplexity. What can be more disheartening to a sincere searcher who is in earnest pursuit of the Holy life?

It is imperative that the heart and mind have a Scriptural unified understanding of that which is basic to winning the Holy life. All too many are not aware that the sure way to hell is gradual. This is the subtle trap in which the Spiritually awakened soul sees himself.

Going through this work step by step will permit the pursuer of truth to know which step he is now on. It is the truth all of us need to face.

"IN THE BEGINNING GOD"

Without God there is no beginning. "In the beginning God," what a foundation upon which to build. There cannot be a beginning without God. It is this Biblical position, not some evolutionary theory, that suggests a big "bang" started everything, or some amoebae emerged from some slime pit and announced it was going to evolve into a being, through a long process until it develops an intelligent man. This takes an enormous imagination that has a faith that can believe that which has no logic or sense.

The Bible clearly gives the account – "in the beginning God," created the heavens and the earth. (Gen. 1:1) All creatures of the land and sea were created, and the majesty of the universe was set in order. And God said: "it is good." God is all completeness. His totality has at His very core, all that He is: Love. Love is never real love in its entirety without its fulfillment being returned with the same surrender and commitment in which God has given. Even though everything that was created was "good"; it lacked the ideal love brings. Since the animals were not created in His image, without a soul, they could not give or return the wholeness the Creator of love entailed or desired. This could only be manifested in that which was created and contained in God's own image. Man became God's necessity, since He wanted to enjoy the rich fellowship of wholly committed love from the crown of His creation.

Once again, God's creative powers reached into the depth of His being to create a human being with this capacity to please His God, and return His love. This potential gives man the power and measure of devotion to adore, worship and glory in his Creator. Man now has all the faculties to respond to what Calvary made possible, and God said: "it is good."

But our God also knew that His love desire could not be accomplished by a dictatorial mandate. For the love that would satisfy His hunger, He must take a dangerous step to make man free to choose to love Him. It is that personal choice that meets man's deepest desire, as well as the yearning of his heavenly Father. Man's freedom of choice is what will give the love God wants to be possible. Freedom, it must be, if man's love is going to please God. But since man is free to choose, he then must be accountable to the Father who gave him that freedom for the decisions he makes each day. His Creator now, through the soul's ingredients, makes man aware of the serious consequences involved in freedom's choices. The soul has a built-in radar, called conscience, when Holy Spirit enlightened is given to lead the way in this awesome responsibility that freedom placed on our door step. In all the Father's Omniscience, He knew freedom was the only way He could receive the commitment that could please the makeup of His being. That God given ability to love in all its purity can only be perfected when choice is free, and the soul is Spirit led.

Because of man's immortality, he must meet God's requirements if he is to lay claim to that heavenly privilege. The immortality God gives, requires an obedience that has a complete and total surrender to God's will throughout earthly life. Disobedience sounds the alarm in the conscience that smites the conscience and will instill an unforgettable warning. This act short-circuits the personal relationship that had been treasured. It blew the fuse, only Calvary's redemptive plan can reconnect the line to the Father. (Gen. 2:16 & 17; Rom. 5:12 & 6:23; Heb. 2:14)

Adam was created sinless to love, worship and glorify his Creator, but chose to use his freedom to disobey and fall from that sinless estate. Man did not stand the test freedom gave, which resulted in Spiritual death. It is imperative we start where man is in his natural sinful condition rather than where we would like him to be. Natural man is lost.

CHAPTER I

LOST MAN
Why is he lost? What is the proof?

The natural questions that man asks about himself are – Who am I? Why am I here? Where am I going? The Bible has all these answers. All beginning is found only in God who had no beginning, nor will He have an ending. Why did God create man, was it not to inhabit the world He had made, and to love, serve, worship and glorify Him in all His Righteousness, Holiness and Goodness? His creation, Adam and Eve were the origin of all mankind, thus, all men have oneness of nature. "And Adam called his wife's name Eve; because she was the mother of all living." (Gen. 3:20) Mankind did not exist before them, and all that come after have their beginning in the Godhead's first human creation – "and God said: let us make man in our image, after our likeness; and let him have dominion over the fish of the sea, and over the fowl of the air, and over every creeping thing that creepeth upon the earth." (Gen 1:26-28) Thus, man was created to live in a higher order than the other creatures of the earth. So with the powers to rule, comes the fact of accountability.

No man, in the final analysis, is subject to anyone but God. "Have we not all one Father? Hath not one God created us? Why do we deal treacherously, every man against his brother, by profaning the covenant of our fathers?" (Mal. 2:10) Paul speaking of the unknown God to the Athenians on Mars hill declared: "And hath made of one blood all nations of men for to dwell on all the face of the earth, and hath determined the times before appointed, and the bounds of their habitation." (Acts 17:26)

This man is immortal. The Proverb writer declares: "The Spirit of man is the candle of God. . ." (Prov. 20:27) This is verified in the human make-up which consists of body, soul, and Spirit. With immortality comes responsibility from which we cannot escape. If man's life stopped with time, he would never have been created in the image of the everlasting and eternal God, because God has no death in Him. There will always be life where God's image is.

Adam and Eve knew the consequences if they willfully went against God's will. It was not as if God had withheld the results of transgressing and tasting what God had forbidden. With this act, inherent depravity entered the human race and is transmitted to all future generations. This fact jumps out at us every day of our life. We are appalled at the depth of wickedness that is confronting our society. It is certain Adam and Eve could not have known the full extent of what their sin would do. It is like the man who takes the first drink. He cannot see himself enslaved by a cruel master that would destroy his manhood; or see himself wallowing in his own vomit in the gutter; or see the fear in his children's eyes if he would happen to appear on the scene. Sin multiplies faster than compound monthly interest. Wherever sin is embraced, it sows devastation with its consuming appetite.

Paul writes to the Ephesian church in these words: ". . .in times past, in the lusts of our flesh, fulfilling the desires of the flesh and of the mind; and were by nature the children of wrath, even as others." He refers to how natural man acts when conducting himself in daily life, saying, flesh has dominion over mind and action. There is within lost man a sense of craving for the forbidden, with the desire to fulfill the lust that pushes the will to act in accord with his unholy appetites. In the mind's laboratory there is a lascivious covetousness that is perverted with ungodliness, and even rebellious inclinations toward Biblical righteousness. Scriptures verifying this truth are numerous, such as Job 15;14; Ps. 14:2, 3; 55:5; 58:3; 1 Cor. 15:22. Each stating that all mankind's depraved nature's will and purpose are self-centered, with a continual bent towards evil. (Evil as declared in the scriptures, and not as the subculture defines it.) Without God there is no standard for right and wrong, thus, no right or wrong, only as the individual views right and wrong in his mind. Without God, men are groping about in their lostness, mired in their night of despair. Nothing irritates the arrogance of self-sufficiency more than to be told all unredeemed souls are lost.

Why did Adam hide from God after he had sinned? He knew he had cut the link willfully and his sin by personal choice had come between the Creator and the created. Sin always blocks God out, and when God is not the decision maker, man walks in the darkness of his own choosing.

How preposterous for the God-man to allow himself to hang on a brutal Cross, if man is not lost! The Psalmist pictured man with these words: "surely men of low degree are vanity, and men of high degree are a lie, to be laid in the balance they are altogether lighter than vanity." (Ps. 62:9)

Because the natural man is lost, he rushes from one thing to another. He always imagines himself to be much better than he is. He is forever trying to find the reason for the rage that the unconquered fury has set off within. The Psalmist asked the same question: "why do the heathen rage and the people imagine a vain thing? (2:1) No one is more tormented with this question than he who knows the makeup of his own heart. The protagonist of desire is clearly revealed in the fruits produced by the sowing and reaping. The cheating on the income tax, adulterating the marriage vows, sitting across the aisle from someone to whom you refuse to speak, hiding a jealousy that has mounted to the point of vicious slander, the fixation with needing to be noticed or appreciated, and much, much more. All these are the fruits of sowing and reaping by the lost soul. This self condemnation breeds soul anguish and a discontentment, brutally ravishing the inner man. The depth of such despair is seen in the mental wards of our hospitals, on the bar stools, in the junkie seeking a fix that will take him out of his present situation, or in the violence of our citizens roaming, and rioting in our streets. If man isn't lost, what is wrong? All of this is enough to cause the angels to hang their harps on the weeping willow tree, and weep tears of shame.

If tears, remorse, social agencies, rehabilitation, clinics, and more laws could have rescued mankind from his inward plight; man's recovery from himself would have happened long ago. In our country alone, we have spent over 5 trillion dollars in these areas, and it is certain this doesn't include crimes, and society's other vices. Money and programs cannot salvage human souls, which can only be done through the blood of the Divine Christ. Did not the Prophet write: "the heart is deceitful above all things, and desperately wicked; who can know it." (Jer. 17:9) We should say, who does not know it?

When Adam sinned, that was mankind's original sin. So the theologians talk of Original Sin, which is defined: meaning the subjective moral state or condition of the head of the human race after failing his test while enjoying his freedom granted in his original holy estate. To describe Original Sin, is to say, it is a fallen state or condition in which man exists outside the Atonement of our Lord Jesus Christ. The depravity that has resulted from Adam's act exists in both the sensuous and the moral nature of man. Out of this nature springs the infection that is now ravishing our world and the individual soul.

Dr. Pope states the effects of Original Sin in these words: "The fall was the utter ruin of nothing in our humanity; only the depravation of every faculty. The human mind retains the principle of truth; the heart the capacity for holy affection; the will its freedom; not yet the freedom of necessary evil. All this we owe to the second Adam." (Pope, compend, Chr. Th. II, p. 52)

If the doctrine of human depravity, resulting from Original Sin is negative, it is because the Bible so states it. "For all have sinned and come short of the Glory of God." (Rom. 3:23). Paul further emphasizes the fact this way: "Wherefore, as by one man sin entered into the world, and death by sin, (that is Spiritual death); and so death passed upon all men for that all have sinned." (Rom. 5:12) Further read Rom. 5:17 & 18; Eph. 2:1 & 5. The Bible is God's monument against man's sin. That is the very reason naturally arrogant people despise the Bible and those who refuse to waver from its standard. Calvary is the extent to which the Triune Godhead has gone to rescue man from his lost estate.

THE HISTORY OF THE CHURCH VERIFIES THAT NATURAL MAN IS IN A LOST STATE.

If we cannot learn the fallen state of man from the scriptures, possibly, we can understand it better from church history, which clearly instituted into its articles of religion the fact that the scriptures teach the depravity of man. Every major Protestant denomination has inscribed in its articles of faith that man is depraved, thus in a lost condition. "For the Son of man is come to seek and to save that which was lost." (Luke 19:10)

The Methodist Church discipline reads: "Original sin standeth not in the following of Adam (as the Pelagians do vainly talk), but is the corruption of the nature of every man, that naturally is engendered of the offspring of Adam, whereby man is very far gone from original righteousness, of his own nature inclined to evil, and that continually." (*The Methodist Discipline*, Articles of Religion, No. VII).

John Wesley attached great importance to this doctrine, which he believed to be fundamental to the Christian Faith by saying: "All who deny this (call it original sin or any other title) are but heathens still, in the fundamental point which distinguishes heathenism from Christianity. But here is our Shibboleth; is man by nature filled with all evil? Is he wholly fallen? Is his soul totally corrupted? Or, to come back to the text, is every imagination of the thoughts of his heart only evil continually? Deny it and you are but a heathen still." (Wesley; Sermon on Original Sin)

No one can be saved until they first realize they are lost. It is imperative a person sees where he is Spiritually before he can properly see his need to be saved. Sin blinds the Spiritual eyes. Spiritual life rests alone in the Divine blood that flowed on Calvary. Robert Lowry, many years ago, wrote these words: "What can wash away my sin? Nothing but the blood of Jesus; What can make me whole again? Nothing but the blood of Jesus."

SECULAR HISTORY DECLARES MAN IS DEPRAVED.

Virgil wrote: "Right and wrong are confounded; so many wars the world over, so many forms of wrong; no worthy honor is left to the plough; the husbandmen are marched away and the fields grow dirty; the hook has its curve straightened into the sword blade. In the East, Euphrates is stirring up the war, in the west Germany; nay, close neighboring cities break their mutual league and draw the sword, and the war god's unnatural fury rages over the whole world; even when in the circus the chariots burst from their floodgates, they dash in the course, and pulling desperately at the reins, the driver lets the horses drive him, and the car is deaf to the curb."

Tacitus gives us his observation of the raw nature man displays: "I am entering upon the history of a period, rich in disasters, gloomy with wars, rent with seditions, savage in its very hours of peace." Again, he said: "All was one delirium of hate and terror; slaves were bribed to betray their masters, freemen their patrons. He who had no foe was destroyed by his friend."

These secular men appear to be proponents of Paul the Apostle as he wrote to the Roman church: "And even as they did not like to retain God in their knowledge, God gave them over to a reprobate mind, to do those things which are not convenient." He didn't stop there, but lands a right cross in a torrent of descriptive adjectives that should make the devil cringe. (Rom. 1:28-32)

Let Mr. Cawley describe Christian Europe in Wesley's day as he saw it: "Man is to man all kinds of beasts, a fawning dog, a roaring lion, a thieving fox, a robbing wolf, a dissembling crocodile, a treacherous decoy, and a rapacious vulture. The civilest, me thinks, of all nations, are those who we account the most barbarous. There is some moderation and good nature in Toupinamboltians, who eat no man, but their enemies; while we, learned and polite and Christian Europeans, like so many pikes and sharks, prey upon every thing that we can swallow."

Has modern technology and conveniences improved the natural nature of this we call man?

"After a talk with Premier Khrushchev, Prime Minister Jawaharlal Nehru remarked to a group of Indians in Moscow: 'once the door of war is opened, life on earth will be completely extinguished. It is strange that when man has the power to improve the lot of humanity and to open the doors of progress, the ghost of war should fall on us. I cannot understand why man should do this.'" (Prophetic Word, Dec. 1961)

Mr. Nehru sees the perverted nature as he tries to work with depraved, lost, self-centered, greedy, power hungry men who strut so proudly in their dark unbelief. Under these circumstances there can not be peace. It is impossible, the human heart will not allow it.

The British press published a letter written by one of Britain's great financiers just before he took his own life.

"On the last day of my life, before my eyes, my brain unwinds the film of the past. In quick succession episode after episode unwinds, and I can now judge that life today is nothing but a human cauldron of greed, lust, and power. Gone are the nice feelings and contentment and in their place is a roaring, hectic existence. I have known to have all you desire, and to have thousands waiting to eat out of your hand. . .From this it must be agreed, that I am entitled to an opinion on life."

The history of natural man speaks for itself, man is lost. He does not seek good only for himself, and prefers that which only involves personal benefits.

ORIGINAL SIN IS UNIVERSAL

Every continent of the world witnesses to the fact that man has a depraved nature and is estranged from the Living God and is Spiritually lost. It can be truthfully said of the unredeemed: "Ye stiff necked and uncircumcised in heart and ears, ye do always resist the Holy Ghost; as your fathers did, so do ye." (Acts 7:51)

John Wesley in his Doctrine of Original Sin pulls examples from various ages and generations in history, not limiting his discourse to any particular locale. He takes further precaution to make sure his samples are not taken from the slum areas.

His first stop is at the Senate in Rome, investigating Cato the Elder, he found this to be true: "When any of his domestics had worn themselves out in his service, and grew decrepit with age, he constantly turned them out to starve." (p. 196)

Speaking of the Asian Continent, Mr. Wesley says: ". . .and call Europe equal either the laziness or pride of the Chinese nobility and gentry, who are too stately or too indolent even to put the meat into their own mouths? Yet they are not too proud or too indolent to oppress, to rob, to defraud, all that fall into their hands. . .Their laws oblige them to certain rules of civility in their words, and actions; they are naturally a fawning, cringing generation; but the greatest hypocrites on the face of the earth." (p. 203)

Wesley speaking of missionary work among the America Indians: "They are likewise all, (I could never find any exception) gluttons, drunkards, thieves, dissemblers, liars. They are implacable; never forgiving an injury or affront, or being satisfied with nothing less than blood." (p. 201)

Being jarred by the realities of what he found in the noble savage, Wesley started to understand empirically the meaning of Original Sin and its impact upon the whole human race. These experiences led him to write in his preface to Original Sin these words: "They that are whole have no need of a Physician; and the Christian Revelation speaks of nothing else but the great "Physician" of our souls; nor can Christian philosophy, whatever be thought of the Pagan, be more properly defined than in Plato's words: 'the only true method of healing a distempered soul.' But what of this, if we do not want a cure. If we are not sick, why should we seek for a medicine to heal our sickness? What room is there to talk of our being renewed in "knowledge" or 'holiness after the image wherein we were created,' if we never have lost that image? If we are as knowing and holy now, nay, far more so, than Adam was immediately after his creation? If therefore, we take away this foundation, that man is by nature foolish and sinful, 'fallen short of the glorious image of God,' the Christian system falls at once; nor will it deserve so honorable an appellation, as that of a 'cunningly devised fable.'"

Anyone who cannot see that there needs to be a radical change in man's nature if there is going be a change in the man, has not been realistic in seeing himself, or honestly knowing people. Only the naive can evade this averse actuality. Children killing children, drive-by shooting without reason, the fraudulent church attender that on Monday morning cheats someone in a business deal, the profane talk show host whose vocabulary is so limited that profanity is common, the lustful mind of the movie producer, the greed of the employee and the employer, the promiscuous life style, the lack of good craftsmanship that covers shabby workmanship, loan sharks found in reputable businesses, and on we could go. Why all this conniving? Because unredeemed mankind possesses a fallen, evil nature, which is evident to any observant human being. In the light of these facts, it is not hard to understand these words: "But they refused to hearken, and pulled away the shoulder, and stopped their ears, that they should not hear." (Zech. 7:11) None of this is because of his environmental condition, but all because of his depraved nature.

Wesley wrote: "Thou ungodly one, who hearest or readest these words, thou vile, helpless, miserable sinner! I charge thee before God, the Judge of all, to go straight unto Him with all thy ungodliness. . .Go as altogether ungodly, guilty, lost, destroyed, deserving and dropping into hell; and thou shalt then find favour in His sight, and know that He justifieth the ungodly. . .The Lord hath need of thee. . .Oh, come quickly! Believe in the Lord Jesus, and thou, even thou, art reconciled to God." (John Wesley, Sermon Five, Part IV, Sec. 9)

WHAT DOES MODERN MAN THINK OF HIS PEERS?

A number of years ago, Max Lerner told the America Historical Association: "For all of its optimism and its cult of action and success, (our) culture has been overlaid with both a sense of agony and a sense of evil." He was giving his estimation of contemporary culture to 1300 college teachers.

Someone else viewed modern man this way: "Our devilish civilization is like a painted face on a balloon. As the balloon swells, the face becomes more and more monstrous, and if we take it at its face value, we will be terrified and paralyzed by it. But actually (and this makes it even worse) it is hallow within. One pin prick and it is destroyed."

The outward manifestation of sin today is bold. It is more than bold, it is obnoxiously revulsive, without restraint, locked in the bosom of carnal man's inner being. What horrors would terrify the unredeemed heart if all the unforgiven garbage and obscenities of the inner life were totally revealed! Paul said it this way: "For it is a shame even to speak of those things which are done of them in secret." (Eph. 5:12) Has it ever, is it ever going to dawn on the human race that, "there is nothing covered that shall not be revealed; neither hid, that shall not be made known." (Luke 12:2) How thankful I am for the precious blood given to cover and cleanse my sins.

Anyone can disregard the facts of man's moral condition, even disagree with the scripture's position of total depravity, but there is no way to escape its truth. For a good many years, especially church attenders, have been conditioned, then brainwashed, misled from liberal pulpits, erroneously devastating and mocking the doctrine of Original Sin, telling their constituents that natural man is basically good. The liberals have said, and still are saying, all man needs is better social surroundings, more education, better medical care, or a more wholesome environment. There is no doubt these things would be helpful, but they will never change what man is on the inside.

Two world wars in a little more than a half of a century, the Korean war, the Vietnamese war, the Gulf war, and the mid-east embattlement that is sitting the world on a powder keg filled with nuclear annihilation, which any one of the numerous conflicts could set off. This should shake up the most arrogant minds of those who dream of world peace, built on man's goodness.

In spite of all this, there has never been a time in the history of our world when more people can read and write; when the standard of living is higher; more and better housing is available. But in our country, crime is increasing five times faster than our population growth. Riots and anarchy are everywhere. Where is that basically good man that is supposed to be evolving into sainthood? Who can deny something is wrong with man that is led by greed and selfishness rather than holy love for God and man?

Even if the Bible did not teach total depravity, history and personal experience have recorded that fact so indelibly that honesty cannot allow this truth to be ignored. No one needs to leave their home to discover this validity firsthand.

There is something in a sweet little baby that causes him after three months on this planet, to get so mad, his face is as red as a ripe tomato. This reveals something that we classify as not the delectable desirable holy love of God. There is no problem to get the child to do wrong, that just comes naturally. The problem is, to get him to do right. A little girl confirmed this by answering: "Why should I ask God to help me be good, when I want to be naughty?"

Every parent can give numerous examples such as the one the minister told about his one-year-old daughter. "She couldn't talk yet but she could toggle around and get into most everything! One day she climbed up and got into the cookies and jam. The circumstantial evidence was all over her face. Yet when he asked her if she had gotten into the cookies and jam, she shook her head no. She couldn't talk, but she could lie. And the worst of it is, they say they get it from their fathers. The truth is, we are liars, just plain sinners by nature.

Even the smallest child can be selfish. One of their first words is "mine." A mulish disposition is natural, and will be anything but Christlike. It is not difficult to find our society polluted with an infectious evil, and its source is natural man. The potential of the disease of this sin-sick soul is alarming and fearful. In himself he has no way to go but to try to find a way to appear respectable, or go down deeper in his materialistic craving to satisfy the basic appetite that dictates what he is. He certainly cannot lift himself by his own moral boot strap.

Sir Oliver Lodge was reported to have said, while he was lecturing in Birmingham, England, as he reached down for a handful of mud: "We have mastered the secrets of molecules, Chemistry, and we are upon the eve of the discovery of atomic chemistry. Probably there is power enough in this handful of mud to lift the German fleet from the bottom of the sea, but I hope it will not be discovered, for we are not yet fit to use it." (Bishop Reed, *Achieving Christian Perfection*, p. 36)

Why would Sir Oliver say such a thing? Because he knew natural man's nature. He had seen it at work and was fearful that lost man would not hesitate to release this destructive power on a world some superman wants to control. Men without God can not be trustworthy.

Professor DeWolf, (his position would speak for most liberals) insists that there is no such teaching, (as original sin) to be found in the Bible. . ." (DeWolf, *A Theology of the Living Church*, p. 198) His Theology persists in making sin come from an environmental accumulation of the past rather than an evil nature. He does not ignore the presence of sin as some, but without saying it, he would like to leave the impression that all we need to do to produce Saints is create a new environment free from the past, and its sins. This alone will guarantee emancipation. The parent was handed a sinful past and from this trap he passes on to his children the same trap his parents gave to him that now has larger jaws and a stronger spring. (See Paul Tillich, *Systematic Theology*, p. 52)

Of course, this can border on fatalism, but I am sure Professor DeWolf, and fellow travelers would be horrified at this thought. His hope, as all, who have undercut the atonement, is in a "new earthly Jerusalem" of social reform, one world government, ecumenical religion, and a planned society under the guiding hand of some brilliant liberal who has the ultimate vision of man's genius. God is somewhere, but who knows where, if He is there at all. Man is adequate for this task. This worn-out theme is still being fiddled by rewording some Biblical terms forced into use, for the purpose of leading a a gullible scriptural illiterate host down doom's path.

Man's violence displayed worldwide has literally rocked the already crumbling foundation of liberalism. Professor DeWolf does a fair job of proving depravity while he is seeking to deny it.

LOST MAN TAKES LEADERSHIP IN THE CHURCH TO DESTROY ITS HISTORIC AND SCRIPTURAL FOUNDATION.

Many of us who were not raised in the church are amazed to find men who were and are placed in leadership and authority positions, are using their influence to destroy the Church's historic doctrines. Historic Christianity finds its most bitter enemy within the framework of the church. It is difficult to believe those who have taken the vows of ordination and declared to uphold the church doctrines, would lie when in their hearts they knew they did not believe them, therefore could not and would not adhere to the doctrines they vowed. This is the worst type of low life, deceptive at the very heart of credibility, dishonest to God and man, a hypocrite of all hypocrites, a manipulative conniving traitor to all truth. The whole objective is to insidiously undercut Godly Truth with half truths and doubt, by classifying themselves as scholars. How can anyone distinguish themselves as scholars and deny the basis of all truth as the correct source on which to build life itself? Anyone to be this devious has to contain a bitter prejudice, which will lead to greater erroneous judgment. But fraud is hidden by a Ph.D, leaning on a professor's desk while ripping the faith from the heart of young Theologians, and passing them on, in their lost condition, to needy imperceptible lost souls sitting in church pews; feeding them ashes, rather than heaven's manna. The Book of Jude clearly details these false teachers.

The pride of lost men fans the passions of arrogant professors and clergymen who refuse to humble themselves to receive God's redemptive Grace. Calvary was totally unnecessary. Of such men, the scripture declares: "seest thou a man wise in his own conceit? There is more hope of a fool than of him." (Prov. 26:12). Isaiah puts a "woe" in his declaration: "Woe unto them that are wise in their eyes, and prudent in their own sight." (Isa. 5:21)

The deceiving false prophets increase as the diplomas increase, sending them on their way to spread secular humanism's gospel, in full contradiction of Bible truth. Charlatan leadership is in the seat of authority that strangles the gospel message. These impostors fully feel they have the truth, and would firmly state they are Christians, in spite of believing that the scriptures should only be considered as just another book. And just because they believe the scriptures as not being divinely inspired, and Jesus only a mere man, no virgin birth, does not mean they are in the classification of lostness as the wine-o in the gutter. In fact, they have come to be our light, to correct our superstitions, placing human reason on the throne rather than a simple faith in the Savior who can save us from sin and our lost condition.

Dr. George B. Foster in his book *The Finality of the Christian Religion* says: "An intelligent man who now affirms his faith in miracles can hardly know what intellectual honesty means." Dr. Foster further claims that: "Jesus did not transcend the limits of the purely human." In other words he is saying, anyone who believes the Bible is ignorant, certainly not a scholar.

It is of this book that a Chicago newspaper columnist wrote: "We are struck also with the hypocrisy and treachery of these attacks on Christianity. This is a free country and a free age, and men can say what they choose about religion, but this is not what we arraign these divinity professors for. Is there no place in which to assail Christianity but a divinity school? Is there no one to write infidel books except the professors of Christian Theology? Is a theological seminary an appropriate place for a general massacre of Christianity doctrine? We are not championing Christianity or infidelity, but only condemning infidels masquerading as men of God and Christian teachers."

They are still among us and growing. Well might the deceivers clothed in their religious garments remember the words of the Psalmist: "Therefore pride compasseth them about as a chain; violence covereth them as a garment." (73:6) Contemptible prophets and teachers live under the religious cloak and rob honest seekers of their place in glory. The highways of life are littered with those whose faith has been shattered by humanism's debasing doctrine. Their faith has been so derailed and crushed, they may never get back on track. This is what they would call man's liberation. They broadcast, Biblical shackles have been torn away and man can now experience real freedom. But no one knows what authentic slavery is until being caught in the web of human reason that can not go any higher than man himself. How pitiful!

C. S. Lewis warned of these professors of religion in these words: "I am trying to prevent anyone from saying the really silly thing about Him, (Christ). Like, I'm ready to accept Jesus as a great moral teacher, but I don't accept his claim to be God. That's the one thing we mustn't say. A man who was merely a man and said the things Jesus said wouldn't be a great moral teacher, he'd be either a lunatic on the level with a man who says he's a poached egg – or else he'd be the devil of hell. You must make your choice. Either this man was, and is, the Son of God, or else he is a madman or something worse. You can shut him up as a fool, you can spit at him and kill him for a demon; or you can fall at his feet and call him Lord and God. But don't come with any patronizing nonsense about his being a great moral teacher. He hasn't left that open to us."

There is nothing so blinding as a religion with no Divine Savior. The terrifying thing is, earnest religious people are lost, if they do not know personally Jesus Christ as their Savior. Human reason falls with man, and all his disdain for Biblical truth will not diminish one iota His Divine validity.

Religious hypocrisy is one of the chief characteristics of how presumptuous so-called intellectuals are who intentionally malign those who refuse to cast overboard their Biblical faith. In fact, their animosity will go so far as to question "the faithful's" intellectual competence, and would suggest as Dr. Foster: "their intellectual honesty." This hypocrisy allows human reason to possess certainties, but allows no such certainties to the soul's demands for the unquestionable certainties of the Spirit, and Eternity.

The floundering of an obviously religious man was clearly expressed on a CBS panel discussion. The subject for discussion was the concern for the ebbing morals of our day. The panel was drawn from the educational, political and religious professions. They spoke with one voice, that in this changing world there could not possibly be any fixed moral code. The religious panelist explained his position in this way : "I have never thought of my God as one with fixed standards for moral right and wrong." He hasn't been reading my Bible. Imagine being in his congregation and receiving this kind of garbage. Just do your own thing, there isn't any right or wrong. These false prophets have done away with accountability and hell long ago.

The result is, our educational institutions have proclaimed the doctrine of no rights or wrongs, even in our Seminaries, until we have a society practicing this anarchy that runs rampant, while our laws which are based on right and wrong are meaningless. When man is left without moral standards or restraints, he becomes a law unto himself. Is this not what we are experiencing now? The conscience has been silenced. Steal, no guilt. Cheat, no guilt. Lie, no guilt. Much of this conscience easing has come from church leaders and educators.

When depraved man is left without God, which means he has willingly left God, to whom he is accountable, out of his decision making, therefore, he is opened to fearful depth of personal corruptness. The German and Japanese World War II concentration camps revealed what a highly industrialized and supposedly civilized people, schooled in scientific technology can diabolically invent. Let gas ovens, mass murdering, and starvation attest to the inhuman depth of viciousness the fallen nature can take the godless soul.

There is no way perverted evil can cover sinister motives, no matter how one chooses to gloss over the reprobate atrocities. Dachau concentration camp is a few miles from Munich, Germany. The buildings are well-maintained and the lawns are carefully trimmed. There are flowers everywhere, and continuing tribute to the thousands of Jews who perished there. Some flowers are in huge urns in front of the ghastly ovens that remain gaping and desolate. A spray of flowers sometimes lies on the stretcher-like trays on which the bodies of the dead were placed and thrust within white-hot ovens. Take a look at the range of detestable horror to which the fallen nature of the human heart can plunge. The ruthlessness of the man who walks our streets is revealed in everyday life. Can any one honestly believe, there is not something radically wrong with man's inner nature?

PROFESSIONAL RELIGIONISTS WALLOW HOPELESSLY IN THEIR SELF-CENTEREDNESS!

Paul warns us with these words: "Let no man deceive you by any means; for that day shall not come, except there come a falling away first, and that man of sin be revealed, the son of perdition." (2 Thess. 2:3)

Professional religionists stand bewildered in the midst of their activism without a clue to the answer for the desperate need of the inner man. With the inspiration of the Bible, Deity of our Lord, and personal accountability under cut, they have no solution. They are forced to the streets to lead some protest, or compelled to startle people by advocating some revolting apostasy, like, "God is dead," or to make news headlines by partying with the homosexuals.

The National conference on Race and Religion reveals their desperation and confusion. A gathering of 1,000 (responsible?) leaders from 65 Protestant, Roman Catholic, and Jewish groups, evidently reached a point of despair in its convention some years ago. What they said then, is still true! One of its spokesman, a former university Chaplain, told the conference: "It is now too late for us to establish harmonious relationship between the races on a world scale." A prominent layman, whom theologians recognized as an outstanding churchman, summed up his view of the matter in this brief sentence: "The most practical thing to do now is to weep."

If these activists cannot "establish harmonious relationship between the races on a world scale," they have no other answer. Is there any way to annihilate the friction between races, when their very natures disallow any such association?

A weak battery illustrates human depravity. There is hope if the battery is connected to the generator, but if not, and it seeks to run on its own, it will not be long before it is dead. If there is no union between the battery and the generator, no matter how strong its beginning may be, it will soon be useless and many times so dead it can not be recharged. Man's Spiritual life can only be found in Calvary's redemptive act.

Germany's scientific age refused to be linked to our Divine God. Human depravity just kept running down. Many of their leaders became dead to Divine accountability, somewhere they were so detached that arrogance drove them to self-destruct. No doubt some became so enmeshed in their pursuit of the super race that they plunged beyond their capacity to return. Their depravity took them out of control and without any moral restraint. History records the breadth and depth of their inferno to conquer the world.

LOST MAN FAILS TO RECOGNIZE THE DESTRUCTIVENESS OF SELF CENTEREDNESS!

The professional religionist can be so absurd, by living in his dream world of idealism, fantasizing that man is not what he is, a self-centered egoistical soul filled with putrid pride. This nasty nature sits on the seat of authority introducing and controlling activities from its cellar. Just assuming this nature is neutral does not correct what it really is.

Those who suggest the nature is neutral must take the position that man is a victim of other people's choices and particularly his own unaccountable decisions. To settle with this belief means that man's nature and his physical body are one. Nothing could be further from the Truth. Man's nature is as much a part of him as his physical body, but entirely separate. The body is the house, while the nature is the seat of authority that runs the house. The body is neutral, which is neither evil nor good. It receives its drive for good nor evil from the motivation of the nature. Everything depends upon the type of nature that is occupying and controlling the body.

On the other hand, man's nature is never neutral. From the first breath of each child, the nature is bent and inclined to evil. Naturally, the pull is away from God and toward self-interest.

THE LIBERAL HAS TROUBLE EXPLAINING THE PRESENCE OF DEPRAVITY!

Some who pose as religious scholars seem to go to the border, if not, into Christian Science to deal with the problem of depravity. They realize something must be done to explain man's downward dilemma. The natural outcome of this position is, man sins because he thinks sin. The mind is sick and needs an adjustment that will deliver him. They fail to realize the nature feeds the mind, and it can not think any better than what the nature allows it to think. The sin problem is centered in the nature and not the mind. When the nature is cleansed, the mind will be healed.

Only the Godhead through Calvary's sacrifice can purify the lust that breeds death to the soul. As in most error there is an element of truth, but mind in itself is not the source of the problem. The dualism of the flesh and the spirit does not make the body and mind evil; everything depends upon the deeper nature, and what commandments it gives.

If you think this is too narrow, read Romans 1:18-32 again. Take the time to evaluate the original Greek for the meaning of each adjective the

Apostle uses to describe the depth of lost man, or just take a dictionary and look up each adjective's definition.

Someone asks, if man is totally depraved how is it that he shows some benevolence in his giving? It must be understood when we speak of total depravity, it can not be confused with total corruption. There is a distinct difference. Total depravity means man's nature is sinful to the extent that it affects his judgment, perception, Spiritual understanding and insight, thus, making it natural to pursue evil rather than purity.

While total corruption means that man has cut all lines with God, has no use for righteousness, is totally consumed with evil and has no desire to be free from its domination. It is a state of corruption whereby there is no road of return.

Dr. Wiley points out how the term total: "is applicable to depravity in three different senses: (1) depravity is total in that it affects the entire being. . .(2) depravity is total in that man is destitute of all positive goal. . .(3) depravity is total in a positive sense in that the powers of man's being apart from divine grace, are employed with evil continually. . ." (Wiley, *Christian Theology*, Vol. II p. 128 & 129)

The false prophet can only leave man at the mercy of himself. Outside of social reform, he has no answer to lost man's greatest obstacle. To avoid the problem of evil man has inherited, is to be guilty of presenting theories and ideas that have no solution to address the basic demand that cries out for freedom from an enslavement that has no mercy. This amounts to refusing to remove the shackles and then casting pity upon his bondage. Lost man does not want pity, he wants freedom, freedom from the depraved nature that holds him captive. Our God has so constituted man that he can not be satisfied with any less. He longs to sing with the song writer, "O glorious freedom, O wonderful freedom," and he can.

PREVENIENT GRACE, THE LIGHT THAT LIGHTETH EVERY MAN!

The foreknowledge of God saw what the plight of man would be after the fall from his holy estate, and refused to allow the crown of His creation to plunge into total corruption. Now He throws the counterbalance into operation by endowing all mankind with Prevenient Grace. John Wesley said: redemption coexists with the fall, but redemption would be of little value to mankind if there was nothing in man to respond to God's redemptive Grace. The image of God in man could only be retained in fallen man by a universal bestowment of prevenient or common grace upon all mankind.

Mr. Wesley describes Prevenient Grace in these words: "Allowing that all the souls of men are dead in sin by nature, this excuses none, seeing there is no man that is in a state of mere nature; there is no man, unless he has quenched the Spirit, that is wholly void of the Grace of God. No man living is entirely destitute of what is vulgarly called natural conscience. But this is not natural. It is more properly termed, preventing grace. . .Every one, unless he be one of the small number whose conscience is seared as with a hot iron, feels more or less uneasy when he acts contrary to the light of his own conscience. So that no man sins because he has not grace, but because he does not use the grace which he hath." (*Wesley's Works*, Vol. VI, p. 512)

The light in Christ Jesus has penetrated every life that enters in to this world. Not one stands without the effects of Calvary, whether accepted or rejected. "That as the true Light which Lighteth (preventing grace) every man that cometh into the world." (Jo. 1:9) By this gift man is prevented from dropping into total corruption, and can respond acceptably to the conviction of the Holy Spirit in his fallen state.

Common Grace is the governing light our heavenly Father has placed in all mankind. It is because of this, he can be law-abiding, honest, charitable and understanding of others' needs. This show of God's mercy is man's prevention from total corruption. The universality of this grace allows it to be bestowed upon the just as well as the unjust. (Matt. 5:45)

One result of this common grace is a conscience, a divine spark in the inner man, which is one of the mediums the Father uses to call man to Himself. Wesley calls conscience, preventive grace, no man, unless he has quenched the Holy Spirit, is wholly void of this grace. It is now accountable man's choice whether to respond to the moving and conviction within. Because of this grace, man has a driving urge to worship. The heathen worship something, because there is something in them that insists on reaching out for the Divine. Only extinguishing the Holy Spirit by blasphemy can annihilate this hunger to worship.

Let it be quickly understood, when we speak of common grace or prevenient grace, we do not mean, "Saving Grace." Common Grace is bequeathed to all mankind, while "Saving Grace" is ONLY given to those who truly repent of the sins, and believe on the Lord Jesus Christ as their Lord and Savior. "He that believeth on the Son hath everlasting life; and he that believeth NOT on the Son shall not see life; but the wrath of God abideth on him." (John 3:36)

Saving Grace is not universally given, in that this grace will save every one, in spite of their willful ungodly unrepented lives. Yet Saving Grace is universal IF every one meets God's conditions recorded in His Word. Then, and only then, whosoever will may come, and will experience God's marvelous forgiveness.

Have you dared to think what would happen in this world if our God would remove all restraints, including common grace and the Holy Spirit? What is left with law and order, would disintegrate overnight. With this world mired in sodomy and greed now, with God's restraints present, visualize the insanity if all reticence were removed.

Thank God that those who refuse to be obedient to His law, still have within them the unwritten law that exposes that which is better than the ungodliness lived day in and day out. Plutarch asks a question many are still asking: "who shall govern the governor?" After some thought he replies to his own question: "Law, the king of all mortals and immortals." Pinder calls it: "that which is not written on papyrus rolls or wooden tablets, but is his own reason within the soul, which perpetually dwells within him and never leaves his soul bereft of leadership."

Common Grace only restrains and can be constantly defeated by motivations instigated by a deviant nature. In spite of this obviousness, common grace still permeates society with a quickened sense of Divine responsibility. This common grace results in man rising to fight unlawful injustice and perform some noble deeds. He can demonstrate anger against grievous inequities, but this will never eliminate his sin problem that is rooted in his nature. Too many good people fail to make the distinction between common grace, and saving grace. And their good deeds and church going can be performed continually without the experience of Saving Grace. The difference between common grace and saving grace is as much as night and day; or eternal life and eternal death.

HOW DID DEPRAVITY COME ABOUT???

Simply stated, man's depravity did not come by accident, nor was it a mistake, as one minister suggested, but it came by a deliberate decision, knowing it to be forbidden. It was an act of man's will, against God's will. That is sin, and always will be sin, thus, Adam as the representative and head of the human race chose to violate God's law. (Gen. 3:6) Yet in spite of that repulsive act our heavenly Father became the seeker after sin's tragedy entered into man's paradise. By choice man lost his original state, and it is only by choice that he can be restored.

Choice brings accountability. Calvary opened the door, for all those who choose to walk in and sup with Him. Try to climb up another way, the same becomes a thief and a robber. This is very insulting to modern man. A man approached a minister and said, he couldn't swallow what he had said about original sin. The minister kindly replied: "There is no need for you to swallow it; it is inside you already." How do we know this is true? By personal experience, by observing others, and the ultimate authority, God's Word.

You can not save that which isn't lost, because the person that feels he is not lost will never respond to Him who can save him. Until a drowning man sees his lost condition, he will never grab for the life preserver I'm throwing to him. But until the moment he realizes the futility of his best efforts to save himself, and clutches the life preserver with a death-like grip and cries: "Save me," he will lose the battle and sink into the sea's depths.

My dear friend, do not expect to be delivered from your sin and yourself, until first you concede you are wholly and entirely lost. This is the first step in finding Christ. It is necessary to start at this point. Lostness brings man under the Judgment of our holy God. Our hope rests in our living Savior.

Barclay in the Letter to the Romans, tells of a young man named William Roby, the great Lancashire Independent, preaching at Malvern. His lack of success drove him to despair, and he wished to leave the work. Then came a seasonable reproof from a certain Mr. Moody, who asked him, "are they, then, too bad to be saved?" The challenge of that sent William Roby back to his work. Paul believed men without Christ to be bad, but he never believed men too bad that they could not be saved. He was confident that what Christ had done for him He could do for any man. (Barclay, *Letter to the Romans*, p. 52)

THE MYSTERIES OF THE INTANGIBLE PARTS OF MAN!

God has made man a very complicated being, burying in his body a Spirit and a Soul; making man both physical and spiritual. With these intangibles He inserts eternity by breathing the breath of life into man's being. Since God is Spirit and the breath of life gave man a living eternal Spirit, now the Spirit allows the desired communication between God and man. The Spirit must contain all of life, both physically and Spiritually. When Jesus gave up His Spirit, physical life departed at the same time. The Spirit is life, containing both physical and eternal life.

Mysteries are only mysteries because they are intangible, but that does not lessen their reality. At the dawn of Creation, God said: "Let us make man in our image, after our likeness. . ." (Gen. 1:26) How can we be made in His image and likeness? Is God saying, we are to look like God? If so, our God would need billions of faces and be made up in different colors. It is evident that this is not the meaning of this scripture. His "image and likeness," is in our spirit and the ingredients of our soul, that incorporates His image and likeness. What God is like, is what the possibilities of our being contains. Jesus said: "he that has seen me, hath seen the Father," Incarnated in Jesus were the summary of our being. He was physical, comprised of spirit and soul.

The Spirit and Soul are cohesive and are mentioned as two entities, yet the Scripture appears to make them synonymous at times. Should one or the other be made primary, since both Spirit and Soul are integrated. God is Spirit, thus, an eternal Being as His presence fills the universe. The soul houses our ingredients that are eternal. The question is, what are these ingredients?

First, what are the most meaningful things in life? Are they not the intangibles? This is not mysticism, but reality. Then the question comes up, how can reality be intangible? There are those who say: "I only believe the reality of what I can see and touch. That is real." Would the questioner deny there is such an entity as love? Can love be put on the shelf for some future use? Can love be grasped out of the atmosphere and held in the hand like a glass of water? But who would dare to say, there is no such invisible quality as love? That which is veiled from the eye is an intricate part of everyday life. How about the intangibles hate, greed, or selfishness. Herein, is the intangible seed that fires the flames that rage into wars where our young men's blood soaks the battle fields of our planet. Do some still say the imperceptible have no authentic place in daily action?

The intangibles operate in almost every area of business life. What happens when you take your money to the bank, and shove your money across the countertop, with a deposit slip, and tell the teller you want that money deposited to your account, and turn and walk out? What did you act upon? Simple faith (the intangible) that the teller was honest, the bank could be trusted to deposit it to your account, so when you needed the money it would be available. Can it be imagined how many times each year, we use, and make, decisions involving the intangible, in operating and controlling our lives?

What does this have to do with the soul? It proves the intangible produces convincing evidence that the credibility of the unobservable is as real as the tangible, and plays a more important part in our lives than the tangible. The intangible is the real person, while the tangible is only the surface of the actual you. The genuine you is inside you, which is unseen by others, only when you pour yourself out. Our God wants to deal with the inside unperishable you. He wants to inhabit the house He gave you, the soul, wherein the undying potential exists.

That which abides in the soul is nourished by the fountain from which eternal life flows. The elements in the soul's storehouse have been placed there as a platform on which man can build for his eternity.

The soul houses God's image. Would our God put His image in some destructible body part, or would He put His image in the indestructible soul? How can a part of God be destroyed? Whatever God creates that has a soul, He must breathe into that being the breath of life. That means this being is eternally alive.

How God will handle His image in the rich man in hell is beyond comprehension. There is the possibility of His removing His image from the lost soul forever, which could increase Hell's torment. But if that be the case, would not removing part of Himself that has life, remove life with Him? If that be so, if God removes life, there would not be any life left in Hell. We know that is not true, because the rich man revealed he had an alive consciousness, with a rational mind, coherent and capable of realizing where he was.

Again, God could leave His image in the unbeliever in hell. Think what the continual torment that would be to know you not only chose this place for yourself, but you also dragged the Holy God's image with you, and now you will forever face it. This I believe is the proper evaluation. Could it be that God's love is so great that He will allow Himself to suffer through His image with each lost soul for eternity. This can be verified by a parent who endures pain and heartache caused by the disobedient child. It would be just like a godly father. The heavenly Father longs for (fully expressed on Calvary) the lost to repent and turn from their wicked ways. He agonizes in pain, but His Justice demands punishment. How can He retain His Holiness otherwise? He must abide by His Word. He said, He is not willing that any should perish, but that all should come to repentance. But when fallen man refuses to repent, God's Justice, out of necessity, must set in.

MAN'S NATURE IS CENTERED IN THE SOUL!

You can't pollute God's image because that is a part of Him, and can't be polluted, but man's nature can be. That is the differences between God and man. Nothing can contaminate God. Man was created to worship and glorify God, and to serve Him with a perfect love. But then man did not stand the test when tempted, and sinned. Thus, man's nature was totally polluted, and the penalty was so grave it opened hell's gates for the arrogant fallen human race. Up until this time hell was only for the fallen angels. By God's foreknowledge, there was a plan set in place to salvage and deliver repenting and believing mankind by the atonement of Christ's cleansing blood. Now man's nature can be restored to the kind of Holiness and purity that our Holy God will accept.

THE MIND IS ETERNAL, THEREFORE, A SOUL INGREDIENT!

There is a definite difference between the mind, stated in the Bible, and the physical brain. The mind is the computer. When God turns the mind on in eternity, man will recall his whole lifetime. God said to the rich man in hell: "remember thy in thy lifetime." He will not forget as he does now. But the physical brain will return to dust. Though different, yet there is a close working relationship.

The carnal mind is enmity against God, because of the damage inflicted by the fall. Paul uses "reprobate" to describe the depth that the mind has fallen, and is not subject to God's law. The mind has motive. Any part of man that maintains antagonism and hostility toward Godly righteousness is wicked. When this is seated in the soul, only a holy miracle can cleanse that mentality. Paul instructs us "to let this mind be in you, which was also in Christ Jesus." The mind sets in motion the conditions of the ruling factors of the soul. In fact the Proverb writer said: "As a man thinketh in his heart, so is he." (Prov. 23:7)

The physical brain is a part of the body which is neutral. It acts upon what it is fed, and has no motive. The brain sends a message to the seat of authority, as to what it sees, what it feels, touches, hears or smells; the message comes back and tells the brain how to respond. The seat of authority makes the decision, the brain sees that it is carried out.

THE SCRIPTURAL HEART IS NOT THE SAME AS THE PHYSICAL HEART, BUT A PART OF THE SOUL.

When the Scripture says: "as a man thinketh in his heart, so is he," it speaks of the life abilities of the soul, where the motivation is. The physical heart doesn't think. It is again stating that there is a deeper part of man than the physical. There is the motivating part that drives the physical. All decision making is entirely initiated at the soul's seat of authority. The true heart is the heart of eternal existence, and is within every soul that ever comes into being. The physical heart is individually possessed. My physical heart may stop, but my Spiritual heart will never stop. Its life is eternal. The heart the Bible sets forth, and the soul could be one and the same, since the soul is the heart of all life in the now and into the forever. The Bible speaks much about the heart, but it is not the physical heart.

THE SOUL HOUSES THE INTANGIBLE WILL!

Over and over again the Bible declares God saying: "I will." God's will is eternal, and our God given will is eternal. Without that will, we could not will our will to our Lord, in order for us to do His will.

When God wills something, He brings together all that He is. Every characteristic of God is fed into His will, all His Holiness, all His Justice, all His Goodness, in fact, every one of His attributes are brought collectively into one, that becomes "I will". He can not will any thing but what He is. God can not will evil, because He has no evil source.

When man exerts his will, he also brings together all that he is, and all that he has received from what the Father has imparted into his life. These essentials become his force that formulates his will. This will can surrender to God's will in obedience, or it can abandon all conscience and Grace to a satanic subculture that wills to destroy all righteousness. Man cannot will anything other than what he is. The only exception is, if he wants the Grace of God to make him more than he is, by surrendering his will to the Savior in holy repentance. When this is done, the will has the capacity for enlargement, to be more and more like Jesus. Man can build on a willing will, everything depends upon whether the source is good or evil.

The angels have a will as eternal beings. Old split foot had to force his will against God's will, before God expelled him to the pit. Satan is still asserting his will to defeat God's every purpose. We can not be any more than what we are, without outside, eternal resources that give empowerment beyond our finiteness. Since the will is accountable to God, it must live eternally with what we are at the point of death, which then will be sealed for all eternity.

It was the prodigal son who said: "I will arise and go to my Father." His will was the force that propelled him out of that pig pen. He willed to leave his father; he must will to come back to the father. The choice was made and initiated the action.

ANOTHER INGREDIENT OF THE SOUL IS PREVENIENT GRACE, THE FAITH NEEDED TO RESPOND TO HOLY GHOST CONVICTION!

This common Grace is bestowed upon all mankind. Without this Grace there would not be anything within the soul to respond to Holy Conviction, revealing man's lostness. This Grace is the counter-balance that keeps man from plunging into total corruption.

Certainly, conscience must be a part of this Grace that awakens to personal accountability. It is also true, conscience can be adjusted over a period of time. At an early age, it can be quickened by the inner two edged sword. But conscience can be hardened by the refusal to obey, and that which pricked the conscience in the past no longer arouses any kind of guilt. Profanity which used to cut to the core, now is used frequently in everyday conversation with no tinge of conscience; taking something from the factory or office which belongs to the company in the preceding years would have caused great pain; but now conscience tells you, you deserve it. Our society is reaping the harvest of a hardened conscience, that tells you anything is all right as long as you can get away with it. Why? Because everybody does it. Man is enslaving himself by his own attempt to disregard the built-in structure our God installed to save man from his personal lostness.

There is nothing so poisonous as a dead conscience that has been conditioned to accept ungodly indulgences under the disguise that society has placed its blessing on rogue indulgence. This daily conscience wall building, can get so thick the soul could not hear God's voice if the heavenly trumpets blasted the message in the soul's ear.

The dead conscience is alienated from God by continual rejection. Each censure turned down drives another nail in Spiritual death's coffin. What a Spiritual death that will be! Yet even terror is mocked because conscience has long since been silenced. No wonder Jesus said there would be weeping and wailing and gnashing of teeth. Such souls should bemoan their lifeless conscience and plead with God to once again tenderize their conscience, and put Spiritual life back in their dead carcasses.

Prevenient Grace has what faith man has, embedded in this Grace. This is the Faith that can reach the Savior, when Godly sorrow is presented. It is man's way out of his lostness.

THE SOUL HOUSES OUR EMOTIONS!

Can you imagine heaven without emotions? Everything about heaven arouses glorious emotions. While hell is described as a place of utter despair and continued anguish, where souls are calling for the mountains to fall on them. Understand, we make the decision now where we will spend eternity. This means we personally choose whether we will have endless emotions that rip the soul apart, or the atmosphere that will be filled with endless praise and thanksgiving for the choices made in this life. Talk about depression and a lamenting hound that is relentless in its agony; hell is that place.

THE SOUL HOUSES OUR MOTIVES!

Motives, which we so desperately would love to hide, have many faces, and can be stashed in many insidious acts. But each one of us will be judged by Almighty God by our motives. The universe is not large enough to conceal even one of them. Our motives are our true person.

Our motive is the motor that drives the will, and maps out our destination. Our motives do encompass our goals, our dreams, either for good or ill. The motive charts the course for time and eternity; superintending each inward action. Since motive can be disguised, the real self is only known to self and the Lord God. Others may never see the real self, for actions do not necessarily reveal the real motive. That action that appears to be gracious and good, may have another purpose in mind.

Holiness is the quest for the innate desire of the soul. Therefore, the motive must be pure at all times. The Holy Spirit is the One who can cleanse and purify the motive and keep it clean, by our obedience. Holiness brings the whole being, body, soul, and Spirit, into oneness. No division is allowed to hinder our relationship with our Lord. The aim is single. The purpose is being holy.

WHEN MAN SEES HIS PLIGHT!

Because man has been given by God the power to think, choose and make decisions, he can not help but look inside himself. Why? He knows there is something radically wrong. His decisions concerning right and wrong are leaving a sense of guilt, in fact, pure misery. They do not line up with what he knows he should be.

The real wake-up call comes when man realizes he is accountable for his freedom. There is something sealed in his soul, that he cannot get away from. He may not comprehend what is happening, but there is a knowledge, he has a rebellious nature that refuses to measure up to what he already knows. It isn't what you don't know that bothers you, but what you do know. This is what is gnawing on the inside, leaving open wounds that refuse to heal. Defy what you will, but there is no way that this consciousness can be denied. That dual nature wars within and no matter what is attempted cannot bring peace. Only a complete surrender to God can bring peace. Without God filling all of life, within and without, there will be that haunting cry: "O wretched man that I am, who shall deliver me from the body of this death?" (Rom. 7:24)

This anguish is a part of man's search as to who he is, and why he is here. And why he can't rise to the lofty height the better inner self wants to achieve. His honest investigation has found the inward problem is so much larger than the outward difficulties. The search will cause him to probe within and without, but if this exploration by-passes the Bible, his pursuit will be in vain. The Bible holds the key to the turmoil that shatters the peacefulness sought.

Everyday life is proof enough, that man is lost, and far removed from the Righteousness that our God accepts. Now, he must find his way back. Hopefully, the following pages will lead this dead soul, buried in enslaved iniquities, into the abundant life.

CHAPTER II

CONVICTION
What is conviction and why is it necessary?

First, we must ask, is it God's will for any individual regardless of who he is, to be lost? Let us allow Peter to answer that in II Peter 3:9: ". . .but (God) is long suffering to us-ward, not willing that any should perish but that all should come to repentance." Ezekiel has God saying: "I will seek that which is lost." Jesus said in Luke 18:11: "Son of man is come to save that which was lost."

It is upon this authority we can comprehend in a greater degree, why our Lord went to the extreme of Calvary to liberate lost mankind. Even now, He pursues the wreckage of humankind. He is the hound that aggravates and badgers the fleeing prodigal. Every devastated dismantled life has left its trail of rubbish that He is following, in relentless pursuit, less the fatal night slips upon you unawares. His heart pleads for you, as your Defender is ready to state your claim before the Judge of all the universe, when you come in true repentance. It does not matter to Him, if life's opportunities have been squandered and substance has been wasted, He wants to set all that right, with His forgiveness that will cast all personal sins away as far as the east is from the west. God's concern and compassion for the lost will never cease. The chase will never terminate until death brings life to its earthly end.

God will use every mechanism He has placed in man, to keep man from plunging into hell's pits. It is at this point the third person of the Trinity, the Holy Spirit, convicts and deepens the awareness of the soul's lostness. This aroused concern comes from Common Grace and the Holy Spirit awaking the soul from its slumber. What man is in his natural state has been uncovered and the discovery frightens the most callous ego, and divulges a heinous self-centered, arrogant person, (himself) that he has seen or met. What a discovery the convicting power of the Holy Spirit has exposed.

The Holy Spirit dares to take this miserable inner self, and hold it up beside the righteousness God expects. How humiliating! Then there is Calvary, that shows to what extent God has gone to deliver from such dreadful peril. Conviction now brings man face to face with himself and His Holy God.

It is evident that many times the Holy Spirit uses circumstances to further penetrate conviction. When flat on your back, and no place to look but up, there is a reevaluation that takes place. It can make one bitter and angry with God shouldering all the blame, or it can crush the ego to the point that it is understood how unworthy one is to be loved by such great compassion. A prolonged dilemma can work miracles when God's rightful place is sought with the whole heart.

This protracted situation can lead to additional conviction as the Holy Scriptures are considered for needed light and guidance. Spiritual eyes are opened, when the Holy Spirit pulls off the blinders. The devil puts blinders on the moral cripples, because he does not want them to get a clear view of just how filthy their pig pen is. We used to put blinders on a horse that was easily spooked, so the horse could only see what was immediately in front of him, and could not see what was coming from the other directions. The devil doesn't want the soul to see anything but the immediate gratification. He doesn't want you to see the final harvest. The scripture details the future for the lost, and the Holy Spirit uses that to put a burr under your saddle, and if it is not attended to, you will certainly be derailed.

If these do not bring Holy conviction, there is this person whose Holy living exemplifies a lifestyle that matches the Scriptural walk. What God said He would do, that is being lived before your very eyes, and this reality can't be denied. You can spit and sputter all your life, but there is no way to contradict what you see. God has His living monuments. They are His Lights.

THEN, WHAT IS CONVICTION?

The scripture uses the word: "pricked in their hearts." It is awakening the soul. It is God moving upon the inner man, arresting, stopping the speeding soul that is going down the road to doom city. What is conviction? Bishop Peck gives this explanation: "Conviction is a law term. It implies the the accused has been arrested, tried, and condemned- - brought in guilty of the of the crime alleged against him in the indictment.

The word has the meaning of an investigating officer, who seeks out the criminal, gathers evidence, questions the guilty, gets verification, apprehends wrongdoers, confronts the lawless with the law.

The Holy Spirit occupies the office of the prosecutor and presents the evidence before the bar of justice bringing to nought every argument or excuse, presses for conviction of the offender and will defend righteousness with endless vigilance

Then the judge must evaluate every piece of evidence, hear every argument, his judgment shall not be defied, nor will it ever be unjust. The Holy Spirit will focus everything upon sin, righteousness, and judgment, in that order.

"Of sin," why, because "they believed not on me." (John 16:9) The rootage of sin is unbelief. Unbelief is inward but also is manifested outwardly, which represents the symptoms that are cradled in human depravity. It is no accident that Jesus used the term sin in the singular. The origin is cemented and anchored in the deviant nature the unredeemed man carries around on the inside nestled in his unbelief. It is the work of the Holy Spirit to uncover and pinpoint this tragic condition of the lost soul.

All too many times the Holy Spirit encounters what the Indian Evangelist did, when a flippant youth interrupted: "You tell me about the burden of sin. I feel none. How heavy is it? Eighty pounds? Ten pounds?" The preacher answered: "Tell me, if you laid four hundred pounds' weight on a corpse, would it feel the load?" "No, because it is dead," replied the youth, and then the preacher replied: "That spirit, too is dead which feels no load of sin." (The King's Business)

The deadliness of sin must be recognized and understood to be the weight that will drag souls into hell. Sin in all its ugly evil, has every right to expect God's Holy wrath.

"But in theology this term has a special sense. It is the work of the Holy

Spirit, imparting to the soul positive evidence of its guilt, its depravity, and its exposures. 'And when He is come He will reprove the world of sin, of righteousness, and of judgment.' So perverted is the natural conscience, that it cannot be relied upon, for accurate moral discrimination for safe and decisive moral implosions, or just and remedial retributions. Man, left to himself, accumulates guilt, with no true estimate of its enormity, becomes harder and darker as crime increases, and treasures up to himself wrath against the day of wrath, and revelation of the righteous judgment of God. The light of reason, or of philosophy shines too feebly to penetrate the gloom of his depravity." (Bishop J. T. Peck, *The Central Idea of Christianity*, p. 30)

In the plan of Salvation, man has a responsibility and so does the Godhead. The Holy Spirit has the charge to convict man of sin; man has the obligation to respond to that conviction in a favorable way. Without the Holy Spirit's intervention man would never fully understand his need for the Savior. If there is no conviction of lostness, there will never be any repentance, no repentance, no Salvation. Understanding this, man does have a part in his Salvation, it is not just in the hands of the Godhead. It is in his choice, and that choice is accountability, which deepens conviction, especially when conviction is considered lightly. Each time conviction is silenced, the next time the conscience will harden to suppress any urgency. Keeping this up over the years, it is understandable how the conscience does not respond. This is the very reason, it is much more difficult for an older person to be concerned about their need to be saved, than a young person. The older individual has had years to build a wall, each year it grows thicker. It isn't that the Holy Spirit is not speaking, but the wall is so dense His voice is not heard. Since the soul is no longer disturbed about the soul's need, its lostness goes undetected. What a sorry state for any individual to be in!

But it is necessary for all to comprehend how serious this spiritual situation is, for once the Holy Spirit convicts the offender, and He is rebuffed; the individual can never be the same. A confrontation with God Almighty is not a trifling matter. This is not mere man that is turning you inside out and upside down, this is your ultimate Judge, which will call for an accounting of that solemn demand on your life. Who can dare to deal indifferently with such a compelling decision? Man's Creator has a rightful claim on each human being that cannot be denied, and this birthright is mankinds whether He wants it or not. It is sealed with our birth, when becoming a living soul with no end. No one can take it away, or act in our behalf. This destiny is left in our hands.

Conviction that is of the Holy Spirit is too profound and engrossed in God's plan that He will not allow the soul to find rest in anything less than completeness in Christ. Man is made to live among the high and Holy, aspiring for that which will count and continue into eternity. How can an extensive endless soul be compensated by fading and momentary things? God has so constituted man that he yearns to be like His Maker. Augustine said it this way: "Thou hast made us for Thyself, and our hearts are restless until they find rest in Thee."

Conviction sharpens the understanding of man's willful disobedience and what it has cost God. Then, man can examine the price personal rebellion is penalizing himself and his influence. Conviction causes the prodigal and the Father to come together, when this is done, there is a soul awakening that motivates man to have an immense desire to make peace with God, to stop running and fighting against the hunger for peace within. Conviction suddenly stops rationalization, and brings focus on the Spiritual interior, and its problem.

Today is the dispensation of the Holy Spirit. He isn't the Johnny come lately. He was active at the dawn of creation, moving upon the face of the deep, (Gen. 1:2); striving with men, (Gen. 6:3) "And the Lord said, my Spirit shall not always strive with man. . ." He who strives with men also departs from men. "But the Spirit of the Lord departed from Saul. . ." (I Sam. 16:14) The Holy Spirit can also occupy men. "Cast me not away from Thy presence; and take not Thy Holy Spirit from me" (Ps. 51:11) ". . .For He dwelleth with you and shall be in you." (John 14:17)

The flood could never have been justified, if the Holy Spirit had not been faithful to strive with men. The corrupt violence of that day (and this day) filled the earth. All mankind seemed to reel like a drunken man. God's Justice demands Justice in the Holiness of pure Righteousness, therefore, adequate striving or conviction has been exhibited, and proclaimed before wrath was poured out. Man's lustful appetites are gathering full steam for that final dramatic event that will close the book on human history, the coming again of our Lord. Who has believed our report? Is our God going to be justified in that cataclysmic moment when He splits the heavens and sweeps the Redeemed into their prepared place, while unbelievers are left for their judgment? This needs to be said again: "He is not willing that any should perish." (2 Peter 3:9) But this is an age that needs to hear Stephen's last encounter with a defiant people: "Ye stiff-necked, and uncircumcised in heart and ears, ye do always resist the Holy Ghost, as your fathers did, so do ye." (Acts 7:51) The ball is in our court, what to do with it is a personal choice.

The wise will honor the Holy Spirit's conviction. The resistance does not need to be an open insurrection against God, but just plain neglect will do the job. Or the disregard can be the fear of men; or the dread of being different; or just the libel of being considered peculiar. The refusal can be any polite rejection denying yourself and taking up His Cross. It all amounts to the same repudiation of the need for God's Grace.

Unequaled patience and mercy still keep the door of Grace open. The scriptures note no difference between what some would dare say are trivial sins that multitudes would love to hide behind, or what these same people would call major or gross sins.

Sin is willful, all sin, is sin in God's eyes.

"Of righteousness" There is no righteousness to which we can truthfully compare ourselves, but His righteousness. Place our sin against His righteousness, it will utterly humiliate the sinner. What man considers righteousness, on the whole, is in stark contrast from the righteousness He sets forth in the Book for mankind. His righteousness demands the perfection of motive, purity of life, Godly virtue, trustworthy character, quality of holy living, sacred honesty, unadulterated consecration, all centered in glorifying God. This is God's righteousness for the human family. His kind of righteousness is the Light that never goes out, and that shatters the darkest night.

His righteousness reproves the world of its unrighteousness. The striking commands of "be ye righteous," "be ye holy," "be ye therefore perfect," "thou shalt love the Lord thy God with ALL. . ." is still in the Book for all to measure themselves. What each person does with its authenticity rests in personal choice, to which all will be accountable at the judgment. There will be all kinds of arguments in favor of a lesser Cross, its message can be ignored for philosophical reasons, but it will still be man's measuring stick by which there is no escape. There is no way to avoid what is, and forever shall be.

"Of judgment," This is an awesome event where everything that is not repented and under the blood shall be revealed. There will be the penalty for the unrighteousness who ignored the conviction of the Holy Spirit, and the acquittal for the righteous, who have believed unto salvation through Christ our Lord. It is at this point when satan's plan shall be destroyed. He now knows his agenda has a final day, and hell awaits him and those who have preferred to grieve the Holy Spirit, and defy God's right to control their life. How can the doom and gloom of that hour be imagined? The unescapable predicament needs Holy Ghost penetration into every lost soul.

Sin and conviction may lie dormant in a hardened conscience, but at the Judgment its ugliness shall be awakened. Multitudes will say, "too late, I should have. . ." Paul cries: "awaken thou that sleepest." The sneers and mocking of the religionist right will be sobering and solemn since there is no way to evade personal choice. Death seals that choice. What has been done with Christ will stand at your side. Judgment will not be a problem, because what each individual is, is standing there with you, and what you are in Christ will make the Judgment, our God will only pronounce the sentence, after the individual has convicted himself.

The Holy Spirit is the ministering Spirit to the whole man with the holy purpose of the Godhead in mind. Man can only find the fullness of himself in the fullness of the Godhead, which makes God and man responsible, one to the other. With conviction comes Light (God's part); with light comes crises; with crises come decision; and with decision comes responsibility; all man's part. Jesus summed accountability up in these words: "If I had not come and spoken unto them, they had no sin; but now they have no cloak for their sin." (John 15:22)

Dr. Ridout in his book *The Person and Work of the Holy Spirit* relates an incident that happened in a church in Scotland that had one minister say in the morning sermon: "if virtue were to appear upon the earth incarnate, ravished by her beauty men fall down and worship her." Another minister spoke during the evening service and said: "virtue incarnate did come to earth, and men's cry was 'away with Him, crucify Him.'" (Ridout, *The Person and Work of the Holy Spirit*)

The cultured man with noble and honest virtues must consider his lostness, as well as the low life violent underworld character. "All have sinned and come short of the glory of God." Thus, all must enter in through His door. Did He not say I am the door, and put the shocker on those who would seek to enter some other way, by calling them thieves and robbers. Rejecting Him, only enhances all other sin in that person's life.

True Righteousness was nailed to the Cross, taking sinful man's place. The bonds of the grave could not keep this Holy Righteousness captive. Eternal Righteousness is impossible to kill. So this Righteousness shall occupy the throne vacated once again. This Righteousness has done all that is necessary for redemption's plan to be completed.

Calvary did not leave this world void of guilt. God could not allow this shame and humiliation to go unchallenged. Such wickedness calls for holy retaliation. God then vindicated this repugnant crime by the Resurrection as the eternal monument of His approval of this Righteousness. There is no way demons can crucify and bury eternal Righteousness, because that Righteousness is life eternal which leaves death and the grave powerless. Our God accepts this Righteousness as the crown for man's salvation. Since our Father has accepted this Righteousness as His standard, it is only reasonable that man should choose the same established premise to anchor his faith. Since Righteousness has come, and is now accessible, man must answer the same question Pilate asked: "What shall I do with Jesus which is called Christ?"

Our God wants to make it clear to all, even satan, what appears to be victory, is ultimately defeat. His purpose is sealed in His Righteousness. It cannot be changed. So watch out you wise men who have filled this world with theories and philosophies, leaving God as a nonentity. This is the same path satan has already arrogantly strutted. O haughty pretensious man, you are on the losing side, following the wrong leader. Your leader will lead you into the pits. This fellow has already received his sentence, final judgment comes at the end of the age.

Materialism has blinded the eyes of the disdainful who have bought into the humanistic religion, claiming man can save himself. History has proven otherwise, even if the Bible is not believed. Multitudes are chained to this world, working on the illusion that wrong can be legislated into right. Effort and time are wasted. No legislation will remove the greed and self-centerness from the human heart. Nothing can take the place of a humble contrite personal repentance before the Savior, seeking forgiveness for a sinful life. The human heart must cry out: "men and brethren what shall we do?"

The sword of the Spirit must wound with the biting anguish that Calvary's experience portrayed. Eternal darkness must be tasted and brought to realization; torment must be heard so memory can record its wails and despair. The soul must be smitten with remorse, knowing mercy will be removed.

Evangelist G. H. Pentecost told of a man who came to see him at a meeting because he was under deep conviction. His conscience was continually condemning him. He was very angry with Pentecost, and with D. L. Moody, who had preached the previous week.

"I wish you and Moody had never come to this city!" he shouted. "Before you came, I wasn't troubled about my sins. You talk of peace and joy but you have turned my soul into a living hell. I can't stay away from the meetings, and to come to them only makes me feel worse. You promise salvation, but all I find it torment. I wish you would leave, then I'd get back my old peace." (Oct. 18 Daily Bread)

All great awakenings carried the piercing knife of the Holy Spirit that was relentless in its convicting power.

In London, John Wesley started his meetings at 4:00 a.m. "A lady became under conviction and could not stay away. When the gentleman for whom she worked heard her stirring in the morning he began cursing and swearing bitterly. His wife said: "I wish thou wouldest go with her, and see if anything will do thee good." He did so. In the first hymn God broke his heart, and he was in tears all the rest of the service." (John Wesley, *Journal*, p. 254)

Conviction will lead to the next step in this ladder to glory.

CHAPTER III

REPENTANCE

What does repentance mean as the corner stone of our Faith?

John the Baptist, our Lord's forerunner, emerges from the Jordan wilderness with this message blazing from his lips: "Repent ye for the kingdom of heaven is at hand." (Matt. 3:2) Our Lord's message does not deviate but is more forceful when He berated Chorazin and Bethsaida with terrifying "Woe" because "they repented not." (Matt.11:20) In Matthew 9:13, He gives the reason for His coming: "for I am not come to call the righteous, but sinners to repentance."

He charges the disciples with the same message when He sent them to the people: (Mark 6:12) Jesus warns the same calamity will come to all generations that befall the Galileans: "except ye repent, ye shall all likewise perish." (Luke 13:3). But He reveals the joy in heaven when one repenting sinner comes to the Savior. This is the result of obedience to the message.

The early church immediately took up the same theme in Peter's post-Penecostal sermon declaring: "Repent and be baptized. . .for the remission of sins, and ye shall receive the gift of the Holy Spirit." (Acts 2:38) The Greek intellectuals encountered the same message from Paul on Mars Hill: "but now commandeth men every where to repent." (Acts 17:30) Through out the Bible, repentance stands at the heart of God's call.

Repentance is that radical reversal from sin to righteousness, which denotes to "have another mind set and a clear cut change of attitude." Any attempt to cover up, or a less than complete turn around, will desecrate the divine mission of the Holy Spirit.

It is making a trivial gesture that demeans the Holy Spirit's work. What dangerous ground to tread. Toying, and being half-hearted with God Almighty, would be like me playing with an Atomic bomb. The bomb is not sacred, but the Holy Spirit is. To scorn the holy Godhead, is a guilt for which I would not want to be responsible when I stand at the Judgment.

Repentance is the cornerstone that anchors our faith. Everything about Biblical salvation depends upon whether repentance is sincere and complete. No genuine repentance, no salvation. Repentance is an unfeigned confrontation with the inner self and the holy God. Whatever Light the Holy Spirit gives must be carried to completion.

There is so much misunderstanding about repentance it is necessary to list a few things it is not.

Repentance is not regret. There are multitudes that regret they are reaping the results of their sin, but refuse to repent and quit the sin business. The adulterer hates the disease that pollutes his blood stream, but not his sin. Judas regretted he betrayed the Master, but hung himself in his despair.

Repentance is not guilt. Hospitals' beds and psychologists' couches are filled, because of guilt. Many come to the altar filled with guilt, and shed tears which is a psychological release and they feel better for the moment, but are soon back wallowing in guilt's pits. Guilt is the knowledge that sin is wrong, and this knowledge tells the person that their accountability will not go away without the Lord God taking it away. Guilt condemns wrong living and improper relationships. Guilt gives no rest and drives many to seek relief or escape in something, narcotics, drink, sex or business. Guilt drove Luther to the Vatican, where he ascended the steps on his knees; Wesley thought he could remove the unrest and guilt if he would come to America and minister to heathen Indians, but left with even a greater weight. There are others who feel that they could eliminate this crushing burden by burying themselves in service ministries, but in spite of endless effort, guilt is still the master.

Repentance is not the conviction of the Holy Spirit lays at your door. Conviction should lead to repentance, but there are those who have been under conviction for the sin that does so easily beset them, still without repenting and turning away from sin to experience God's saving Grace. Felix trembled under conviction; Agrippa was almost persuaded, yet there is no evidence that either one found Christ who alone can save. It is the enemy's trap to confuse conviction with repentance. He fears the soul that truly repents.

Repentance is not that fear that invades the mind in that lonely hour. There is the fear of God's wrath. Satan himself fears that horrible hour when that wrath will be poured out upon him and all who followed so faithfully.

Fear gripped the heart of Belshazzar and all who were with him, as all watched the great king seized in utter terror. He sensed judgment, because he had lifted up himself against the Lord God. Imagine seeing the hand of God writing your death announcement when revelry was at its height, and the living God was without thought. What terrifying words reverberated through the palace: "Thou art weighed in the balances, (God's balances), and art found wanting." This unexplainable gripping fear saturated the very atmosphere. Where was the power of that blasphemous king now: "his countenance changed, and his thought troubled him, so that the joints of his loins were loosed, and his knees smote one against the other." (Dan. 5:6) All the fear that the human body can absorb is not repentance. No matter how deep the fear of God is, it is not repentance. It may lead to repentance, but in itself it is not repentance.

Repentance is not mere believing. The demons from hell believe. How does man, who professes to be a Christian answer when asked, do you believe that Christ is the Savior, or do you believe the Bible to be the word of God, or do you believe there is a heaven, and there is a hell? Without doubt almost all would answer yes. Yet, they practice sin openly. But they said they believe in these crucial questions asked.

Annias and Sapphria did believe. People do not give half of all their possessions without considerable Faith in the cause to which they are so generously giving. It is next to impossible to get the average professing Christian to tithe their gross income, let alone, give one half of their possessions. But they lied, by giving the pretense they were giving all their possessions. There evidently was no repentance, and they fell dead at the disciples feet.

It is disheartening to find those who are working with seekers to emphasize believing in the Bible, that Christ died for them, and etc. There is nothing wrong with this, but little or nothing is said about repentance, that may include restitution, or making a relationship right by asking forgiveness. If repentance is not complete, and genuine, and willing to forsake all sin, now and forever, what good is believing all the necessary things mentioned? It is certain, orthodox believing is not enough for an individual's salvation. Repentance is the basis on which your believing will then produce saving faith.

Our Lord's command was and is: ". . .except ye repent, ye shall all likewise perish." (Luke 13:3) Repentance is the key. Our Lord puts repentance in direct line with a soul being saved or lost. Repentance is the primary principal in salvation's plan. "Except ye repent" is a condition that must be met before salvation is available. Wrongfully people are being taught that believing is all that is necessary. It is utter futility trying to believe in Saving Faith if there is not a willingness to forsake the pet sin or sins.

This lack of instruction is the very reason there is no depth, and an eventual falling away. There is no way that two masters can be served. While in Japan, an equivalent to our school superintendent came forward for prayer. He was not getting anywhere, finally through my interpreter, he asked, "can I have my Buddha and Jesus too?" Here, we ask, "can I have my sin and Jesus too?" The answer is the same. All Buddha's and sin must be abandoned or there is no salvation no matter how hard the believing issue pressed.

Repentance is not confession. Satan does not mind if sin is confessed, that relieves some guilt and conviction, but if sin is continued, why bother. Many confess only because they are caught, others because regret is only for the moment, others confess to get approval, but if confession is made without absolute repentance, no matter how long you stay on your knees and acknowledge personal sin, the effort is useless. Confession is used as the Catholics practice the doctrine of penance.

Perhaps your child has broken the home rules again and again, and each time asks for forgiveness, by promising he'll not do it again. But he continues to breaks these rules daily. It finally dawns that confession is no more than a way to get out of the trap. Soon these confessions are meaningless. He has no intention to truly repent and forsake his wayward ways.

Many people live their whole lives this same way and actually feel they are Christian because they have confessed their sins. Repentance is a termination with willful sin, while confession is only an acknowledgement that you have sinned. If there is no repentance, confession is worthless.

Repentance is not meekness or humility. These are God given graces that too many substitute for repentance. An easygoing, kind and sympathetic disposition is a gift from God, but it also can be a stumbling block to salvation. All natural goodness is as filthy rags. There is quite a difference from that impulsive individual who blurts out, or is pushy. But both must travel same route if they are to experience salvation.

These few things are listed to make us aware of those who would make them equivalent with repentance, so they can evaluate what true repentance is. It is the cornerstone of our Faith. Without it being placed in the right place, our Faith will crumble and fall.

THEN, WHAT IS REPENTANCE?

It is one thing to hear about repentance and even declare it, but quite another to repent. Repentance is man's part. Only man can turn from sin to the Savior. The Lord will never doing the turning for anyone. The Lord has put it this way: ". . .yet if they pray toward this place, and confess thy name and TURN from their sin, when thou dost afflict them; then hear thou from heaven and forgive the sin of thy servants, and thy people Israel. . ." (2 Chron. 6:26 & 27)

Repentance is not only for the moment, but if it is genuine, it will continue day in and day out. One never stops turning their back on sin. This is why repentance is the cornerstone of our Faith. The instant we stop, we allow ourselves to be open to committing sin. Then there will be no basis of maintaining personal salvation.

Saul experienced this on several occasions. Samuel explained what God's will was before he went into battle with the Amalekites, but he felt he could go three-fourths of God's way and the other fourth his own way. The Amalekites had some mighty good looking sheep and oxen. Even though God said he should do away with them, he felt it would be a shame to slaughter them. God said to Samuel: "for he is turned back from following me, and hath not performed my commandments. . ." (I Sam.

15:10) God wants utter and complete obedience, nothing has changed since the time of the initial repentance. Saul's whole life is an example of this man's failure to carry through that which he once resolved to do when he repented. This is failing, at the point of his probation.

Repentance is then turning 180 degrees away from all willful sin and pursuing God's will only. What is willful sin? It is exhorting your will against what you know to be God's will. Repentance, in its full meaning is refusing to go against God's known will.

Archbishop Tillotson suggests that in all too many cases "their repentance is too late." Too few repent of showing partiality, gossiping, backbiting or speaking disparagingly when that person's back is turned. (Isa. 58:1-12; Ps. 15) There are these annoying and will reinforce the fact that the will of God is known, while ignoring the correcting of the Holy Spirit. All too many are perfectly satisfied with the state in which they find themselves, but totally oblivious to their fate. "The darkness which covers him on every side, keeps him in a kind of peace. He sees not that he stands on the edge of the pit; therefore he fears it not. He cannot tremble at the danger he does not know."

No one will thoroughly repent, if there is not the feeling of the weight of sin's curse. Repentance is more than accepting Christ, being baptized and joining a respectable church. It is absolutely loathing the inner self that embraced sin and its shame. Sin destroys personal Faith that longs to be wholly committed to God's perfect will. Repentance is the right about-face from the old sinful life, to the new life in Christ Jesus, which demands total obedience from mind, body, and soul.

Have the Lutherans sidestepped repentance to emphasize Justification? Have the Reformed Theologians ignored repentance to stress the decrees? Has Catholicism covered repentance under their doctrine of penance? How about the Protestant masses and many evangelicals included, who have cheapened repentance to mere confession?

Without understanding the depth of requirement for repentance, it could mean the differences between Spiritual life and spiritual death. Repentance brings the soul to the crossroad of what he is going to do with Christ. There is a very definite choice made concerning "whom will you serve?" Repentance must be complete because it is the primary principle on which you must build Faith, if this step is not forthright, no one can advance successfully Spiritually beyond this point.

There is more spiritual fraud at the point of genuine repentance than at any of the other steps of salvation. What is it that deceives multitudes from thoroughly repenting?

The liberal has boasted: "we have gotten rid of the troublesome way of repentance." Indeed they have, and droves of gullible people who seek an easy road are rushing to their spiritual doom. The church has no influence on society's affairs because we have made our foundation (repentance) a matter of personal opinion. Repentance is made to mean anything the individual may want it to be, taking it out of its Biblical context. How bold unregenerated man is when he can trample and crush Biblical standards to suit himself.

While the Prodigal son was in the pig pen's filth, there could have been numerous confessions, many prayers, even open acknowledgement that he had done wrong and sinned against the father, but if he stays in the pig pen, he will continue without the father's forgiveness. To truly repent, he cannot stay in the pig pen,

Under the compulsion of Holy Ghost conviction, and prevenient Grace, he was able to look at himself and see the mess he had made of his life. The scripture says, he came to himself, and cried: "I will arise and go to my father." You are seeing true repentance in action, as he gets up, climbs the fence and turns his back on that filth in which he was wallowing, and all its so-called pleasures and headed to the father. He left the father by choice, he must return by choice. He found the father right where he left him. The heavenly Father never leaves us, if there is any leaving to do, we are the ones who will do the leaving.

Manual Article VIII states: "we believe that repentance, which is a sincere and thorough change of mind in regard to sin, involving a sense of personal guilt and a voluntary turning away from sin, is demanded of all who by act or purpose, become sinners against God. The Spirit of God gives to all who will repent the gracious help of penitence of heart and hope of mercy, that they may believe unto pardon and spiritual life."

Repentance carries with it an absolute determination to love God at all cost. It is impossible to fall in love with our holy Father and have others lovers at the same time. This love is not only vertical but also is horizontal, which includes daily relationships. Can we not say that repentance must stand for absolute integrity? All answers will be yea or nay. There will not be any shaving the corners. The will says, from this day forward, I will only serve the living God. This is not intended to imply that the will in itself has all the power needed to pull man from the pig pen, but the will allows the activation of Prevenient Grace and Holy Spirit conviction to undergird the willingness to make the break with sin and satanic enslavement. Operating together, the resistance of the depraved nature, when placed at the foot of the Cross, can no longer maintain its strangle hold. It is no match for the power Calvary now releases.

The will now understands God's attitude towards sin, and is willing to let God's will be the ruling factor. For the first time, sin against the Savior is seen in its true light, as an abomination, a repulsive insult to our holy God. Repentance will never go to the depth it must go, if there is little understanding of how despicable sin is. Would our Lord allow Himself to be hung on a Cross for some insufficient misdemeanor? Sin and the lostness of man were of such dimensions that nothing less than the shedding of Divine blood would be adequate to atone for its curse. How hopeless man would be without the Savior's intervention.

Wesley says it simply: "by repentance I mean conviction of sin, producing real desires and sincere resolutions of amendment." (Vol. VIII, p. 428) There is no way our Lord can repent for us. It was not His choice. Thus, the forsaking from sin must be a choice of will.

"Repentance, like conversion, is generic, comprehensive in its character; it covers sin as sin. It is impossible to repent of a particular sin without repenting of sin as such – of all sin. The repentance may begin with a particular sin that is of the carnal mind which is the essence of all sin – hence in repentance it can not be necessary to recall every past sin; such repentance would be impossible. The sinful mind, the self-indulgent will, is renounced, and thus all sin is repudiated, even if a particular act of sin be not at the moment recalled." (Fairchild, *Elements of Theology*, p. 250)

Repentance is the disposition of heart which moves God's heart to receive the seeker that has thrown down his rebellious weapons, forsaken ungodly appetites and prides, turned with a broken heart to Him who the will has chosen for time and eternity regardless of the denial involved."

Somewhere I read these words: "Repentance cancels judgment. Two-thirds of the apocalyptic judgments are meant to be remedial, for they are punctuated with the refrain: 'and they repented not' (Rev. 9:20). It is only during the final third that the refrain disappears and the judgments, like hell, become purely punitive."

True repentance must involve restitution. Mr. Finney said, the thief has not repented who keeps the money he has stolen. Repentance involves facing up to the responsibility of making wrong right whereever it is possible. The thief needs to go to the one whom he has wronged, restore the money, and make necessary restitution, with a clear declaration that he is through with all thieving. When this is done, he is in the position to move forward Spiritually. Too many have not found victory because they have refused to face unrepented sin and walk in the Light the Holy Spirit reveals.

A married woman tried to commit suicide when she found out the man with whom she had had an affair for 9 years was going to marry someone else after his wife died, because he could not conscientiously marry a divorced woman.

He sings in the choir and teaches a Sunday School class. He lives as if he is above the consequence of his hideous sin.

The lady involved found the Lord, before her husband and pastor and his wife, she came clean and found peace with her Lord. It was a must. There are no shortcuts for the seeker. Repentance includes everything.

What about the man? Like so many, there is an attempt to ignore and push aside the ugly sin, feeling repentance is not necessary. How miserable such a soul! How can any one find God, if they don't make wrong right, if it is possible.

Repentance requires more than restitution. There is an obligation to the individual not only to make wrong right, but to try and put that person where he or she would have been if the reputation or article had not been stolen in the first place.

To sum up repentance, Dr. Wiley has this to say:

"We may say then that repentance implies:

(1) A conviction that we have done the things we ought not to have done, and left undone those things which we ought to have done; that we are guilty before God and if we die in this state must be turned into hell.

(2) That repentance includes contrition of sin, and that the remembrance of sins will always be grievous and the burden intolerable;

(3) That true repentance will produce confession of sin;

(4) That true repentance implies reformation, a turning from sin to God and a bringing forth of fruits meet for repentance. It is for this reason that Mr. Finney defines repentance as a turning from sin to holiness, or more strictly from a state of consecration to self, to a state of consecration to God; while Dr. Steele says that 'Evangelical repentance is called a repentance toward God because it consists in turning from sin to holiness, implying a sense of, and hatred of sin and a love of holiness.'" (*Wiley Christian Theology*, Vol. II, p. 362)

Repentance moves the seeker to the next step, confession.

CHAPTER IV

CONFESSION IS NOT FORGIVENESS
When is confession genuine?

Modern day religion makes confession, repentance and forgiveness all one. And some make confession an end in itself. One minister prayed, "forgive the sins that separate us from God, forgive the sins that separate us from each other." With one mighty sweep all sins were to be forgiven. The very words intimate all are living in willful sin, so all is forgiven, come back next Sunday, and we will then confess your willful transgressions again.

Saul thought the same way; "and Saul said unto Samuel: 'I have transgressed the commandment of the Lord, and thy words; because I feared the people, and obeyed their voice. Now therefore, I pray thee, pardon my sin, and turn again with me, that I may worship the Lord.'" (I Sam. 5:24 & 25) He got caught. The very reason he is confessing now, but he never honestly repented, finally committing suicide on the battle field. Confession is without worth if there isn't wholly repentance, nor is forgiveness a reality, if genuine repentance does not precede confession, that will bring forgiveness. It just does not work any other way.

Because of this erroneous teaching, our people subconsciously believe and hold, that salvation from all sin is impossible. (I John 1:7) And any hope of heaven is bound in one continual confessional. The Bible teaches that any willful act of disobedience against God or man is sin. Sin disconnects man from God, and unrepented sin means man is left without hope. Notice, I did not say confessed sin, but it is unrepented sin that will face hell's fiery pits. The problem is not confessing sin, that is one of the more easy tasks, but complete repentance is the key. Confession without true repentance is no more than a sounding brass and tinkling cymbal. A weekly confessional, for past sins that there is no intention of quitting, and will be continued the coming week, is bordering blasphemy, and shamefully degrading to Truth. This stands to make a mockery of His precious blood that cleanses from all sin.

Our people are schooled in a defeated religion Sunday after Sunday with the confessional prayer like the following.

"Our heavenly Father, who by Thy love hast made us, and through Thy love hast kept us, and in Thy love wouldst make us perfect, we humbly confess that we have not loved Thee with all our heart and soul and mind and strength, and that we have not loved one another as Christ hath loved us. Thy life is with our souls, but our selfishness hath hindered Thee. We have resisted Thy Spirit. We have neglected Thine inspirations. Forgive what we have been; help us to amend what we are; and in Thy Spirit direct what we shall be; that Thou mayest come into the full glory of Thy creation, in us and in all men, through Jesus Christ our Lord. Amen."

Sounds humble enough, but what an absolutely defeated Spiritual life is portrayed. God has called us to "Be holy, as He is holy," but He can't realize His purpose because all, saint and sinner alike, refuse to do His will; His commandments are not kept; selfishness and self-will dominating; the Holy Spirit is resisted; the Bible is neglected; and we are asking the Holy Spirit to direct us, but He can't because we resist Him. Talk about a defeated religion that is at the mercy of sin, here it is, and being promulgated week after week. This is a sinning religion that only advocates a confession of sin, with no forgiveness at all, Forgiveness is forgiveness from sin, a deliverance from sin, not a forgiveness in sin. The Book says only the pure in heart shall see God. The commandment is to love your neighbor as yourself and love God with all your heart, soul, mind and strength, and then He reinforces this by saying; "if ye love me keep my commandments." Does not that mean, continually each day and night? The love of God does not allow sin to reign in us at any time.

Luther was seated in the Confessional at Wittenbury, listening to many of the townspeople confessing of great excesses of sinful living, adultery, licentiousness, usury, ill-gotten gains were all acknowledged. He reprimands, corrects, and instructs. But to his astonishment when these individuals replied that they would not forsake their sins.

Greatly shocked the pious monk declared that, since they will not promise to change their lives, he would not absolve them. The unhappy sinners then appeal to their letters of indulgence; they show them, and felt these were adequate to maintain their virtue. But Luther replies that he has nothing to do with these papers and adds, "Except ye repent, ye shall all likewise perish." They cried out in protest, but the good doctor was immovable. They must cease to do evil and learn to do good or else there is no absolution.

A soul that sins shall die, and a soul that confesses, and keeps on sinning shall die. Therefore, these confessional prayers are contemptuous and vain if they are an end in themselves, and willful sinning continues. Has any soul repented who continues on in willful disobedience? It is thumbing your nose at God's commandments and the price He paid to deliver each soul from all sin.

It is true that confession is an acknowledgement of our accountability to God, and His sovereign right over the human race. It is further true, that confession, when genuine repentance has been completed, is the key that unlocks the inner chambers of forgiveness.

When confession has all the elements of real repentance; forgiveness, and cleansing will be experienced and the soul will not stumble as it proceeds to advance to each step of this glorious salvation. (1 John 1:9) The vertical and horizontal Spiritual dimension has a complete function when each step is obediently fulfilled.

Some will deliberately or innocently misunderstand this position. Rev. Jack Ford clearly discusses the subject in the following words:

"Yes, it is clear that if there is a lapse of faith or obedience it must be confessed, and forgiveness and cleansing sought. But is this the place that confession has in the prayers and the worship that he had notice that little or no place was given to confession of sin in the prayers that were offered at the holiness meetings he attended. To many this will seem a glaring omission, and a word of explanation is not out of place.

"Firstly, the holiness people believe that when we are justified by faith God 'removes our transgressions from us as far as the east is from the west.' (Ps. 103:12) To ask for the forgiveness of past sins is to cast doubt upon all the great and positive promises of God. Why ask for what is freely granted and sealed with the blood of the Son of God." (*What The Holiness People Believe*, Jack Ford, p. 65 & 66)

Some say there is a need to confess what is called "the sins of ignorance." Ignorance is a lack of insight, unaware because of being uninformed, but where is the will that was willed against God? Without doubt our limitations, since we are not God, can display ignorance unknowingly, but honest ignorance, cannot be classified as willful disobedience. If Spiritual Light is focused on an area of past ignorance, it is no longer ignorance, but placed in the area of accountability. But a lack of Light is not accountability. How can you honestly confess that which you don't know. Yes, you can but ignorance is only enhanced because their is no understanding as to why it is being done. The unknown sin can be sin, but how is the unknown understood to be sin if it is unknown?

There is a psychological release that comes with any confession, regardless of how shallow repentance is. Most people find it much easier to confess their sins, than to repent and forsake their sins. Because this confession gives a certain relief, it is mistaken for forgiveness. A murderer may find the torment of his guilt lessen by confessing, but can still retain a murder's heart. Again, confession without forgiveness.

The act of Communion and taking a gift to some needy mission project, becomes penance for many church members. Acts like this apply a special refinement to a proud rebellious heart to release some guilt. Such a person has no intention to adhere to the Biblical meaning of the Communion, or to fear receiving it living a sordid life, harboring willful sin.

Communion Sunday came and the confessional was omitted. This dear lady was deeply disturbed and did not mince words telling the minister about this unforgivable neglect. It was impossible for her to take Communion without confessing and bewailing her manifold sins. Her carnal anger was evident that across the years this type of confessing had not done a thing on the inside to rid her of the explosive anger she vented on various occasions.

Paul writing to the Corinthian Church instructs them concerning this matter: "Where-fore whosoever shall eat this bread, and drink this cup of the Lord, unworthily, shall be guilty of the body and blood of the Lord. But let a man examine himself and so let him eat of that bread and drink of that cup. For he that eateth and drinketh unworthily, eateth and drinketh damnation to himself, not discerning the Lord's body. For this cause many are weak and sickly among you, and many sleep." (1 Cor. 11:27-30)

Who then is worthy? All who have genuinely repented, and through Faith been Justified by the Lord's gracious act of forgiveness; sins under the blood, and living moment by moment in obedience to God.

The early Methodist class meeting was a revival of the New Testament church dynamics. Of late there has been some renewed interest in this informal approach to mental therapy and psychological problems. There is a great difference. One is used as a release from bondage mentally and physically, while the New Testament church and the Methodist class meeting dealt with the Spiritual need. These were like-minded people who came together to share their spiritual victories, temptations, and to nurture those that felt they had lost the victory.

Yes, there were times of opening up the inner man and revealing the anxieties, burdens and temptations, but this was not used as a confessional. These were praying people who knew how to take every need to God. These like-minded people believed in miracles and were unified in Faith that could remove mountains if necessary to solve problems and give victory over temptation. Here, each soul found a love bond that is superior to anything else in life. It was said of the early church, "behold how they love one another".

If there were those who dropped into Spiritual laxity, the fervor and love of the group, brought conviction and gave the wounded soul Spiritual undergirding, enabling them to pray through to Spiritual victory. It was not the intention of the group to be a crutch or a confessional but to give spiritual strength and reinforcement. The church at its best, is one great mass moving and loving in the field of Holy dynamics. Its power is gone when it deteriorates into nothing more than mere confessionals.

Confession is baring the soul before our Holy God, and if necessary before men. Soul sickness requires a valid cure no matter how unpleasant it may be. This confession must reach to every unexplored depth of the soul and necessitates the foul filthy ungodly sludge and slime be expelled by the Savior's Justifying act. Since the soul is to be Spiritually whole, and healthy which will take on God's nature, everything repulsive to His Holiness must be evicted.

Actually, true confession is vomiting up all the rotten known sin. It is Spiritually rebelling against all impurities within. It takes on an utter distaste, and abhorring of that which was once embraced.

H.W. Beecher said: "A man will confess sins in general; but those sins which he would not have his neighbors know for his right hand, which bow him down with shame like a wind-stricken bulrush, those secret sins, he passes over in his public prayer. Men are willing to be thought sinful in disposition; but in special acts they are disposed to praise themselves. They therefore, confess their depravity and defend their conduct, making themselves to be wrong in general, but right in particular."

CHAPTER V

SAVING FAITH

What is the difference between Saving Faith and Faith?

A soul seeking our Lord with all its heart moves from confession to Saving Faith quite naturally and quickly. This type of Faith gives God's word action. "And Jesus said unto the centurion, go thy way; and as thou hast believed, so be it done unto thee. And his servant was healed in the self same hour." (Matt. 8:13)

The faith exercised by the centurion was Saving Faith. A definite distinction will be made between what is generally referred to as most religious peoples' faith and Saving Faith. Jesus said: "according to your Faith be it unto you." (Matt. 9:29), which would indicate there are degrees of faith. The eyes of the blind were opened by their faith. On the other hand, the rich young ruler walked away when confronted with the faith to sell all. His faith allowed him to keep the commandments, but there was not enough faith to sell all his riches (his real god), and follow the Savior. His faith did not and could not cover the gloom that swept across his soul. His faith only gathered darkness when faced with the Faith that demands ALL. The rich young ruler's faith is verified by multitudes who sit in the average church pew each Sunday morning.

Some thinking individual is bound to ask, is Saving Faith the gift of God or does man have a part in this phase of his salvation?

One far greater than I has declared that Saving Faith is the sole gift of God, even my beloved John Wesley. I shutter when I dare to question such a spiritual giant of whose shoes I am not worthy to unloose. But if Wesley is saying: faith is a part of prevenient Grace, which is God given, we can agree. But this faith, is not Saving Faith, it is common grace given to all mankind. This faith in itself does not save. If that were true, there would be no need for Calvary.

It is true, the Holy Spirit and Common Grace come together to convict the lost of their sinful condition, and move the convicted ones to respond to the impelling pull of the Savior. In all this inner persuasion and convincing thrust the individual's will must be activated in action. Only man himself must have the want, too. Saving Faith cannot be ignited until man surrenders his will. When the will's Faith relinquishes, and says, I want this more than any thing else, this faith now has God and man pulling for one thing; the removal of all knowing sin. The soul is leaping towards its only hope.

Someone gave this account of a lad who asked the question: "How can I be saved?" The person whom he asked, told him he would show him. He proceeded to set a tub of water on the ground and instructed the boy to kneel beside it. He then placed his hand on the boy's head and forced it under the water and held it there for a short time. When he released the boy he came up sputtering and gasping for air. He then told the boy that when he willed to be saved as much as he wanted air, then he would be saved.

Where does this will that wills its faith, have its origin? Since our God will never force our will, it must come from within in response to the arousing conviction of the Holy Spirit and Prevenient Grace. Is not this passionate yearning for God housed in the soul? It is true that the will in itself will never be sufficient to bring about Spiritual transformation. The will has no supernatural self-generating power. The will on its own will fail, but when brought together with God's agencies, Saving Faith is the result. This is not implying salvation is the consequence of man's effort alone. Never!

The point is that man must have a completely submitted will that allows his faith to respond to the Lord for the deliverance from sins. The gift of salvation is only given when God and man will it so. Otherwise, there would appear the necessity of predestination.

Everything of eternal worth is the gift of God, which also includes man's soul. Freedom is one gift He has given, which allows man to operate these gifts and be a moral being honoring the Giver, if not, He would be a mere machine, without responsibility for the gifts at his disposal. His freedom allows him to will or not to will to use these holdings for God's glory.

Saving Faith through the act of the will is a response to God's love under His conditions. If Saving Faith had its source entirely in the Godhead, this would leave man without accountability. Faith must flow from a source to a source to be faith. Just as love would never be love without it being given and then returned. Faith cries out: "God is everything, I am only a lost sinner. I want forgiveness from the living God, and in turn I'll give myself to be used as He sees fit. God gives, I give. It is a two way street. A one way street ends up in nothingness. God does not respond to Himself, but He does acknowledge and return forgiveness to the abandoned self will.

Common Grace, initial preliminary faith, and Holy Spirit is God's part in Saving Faith, while man's part rests upon the will and whether it will submit to God's will and purpose for one's life. If Saving Faith is to be obtained, the personal will always obey.

Dr. Williams points out, Wesley gives two movements of faith that is to lead to Justification. "Preliminary faith, which includes the free response to God's prevenient Grace and a desire to please Him but is still only the 'faith of a servant.' Justifying faith proper, which is a sure trust and confidence in Christ bringing a conviction of forgiveness, this being 'the faith of a son.'" (Williams, *John Wesley's Theology Today*, p. 65)

Before Wesley's Aldersgate experience, preliminary faith was the extent of his spiritual knowledge. In spite of this, there are very few whose labors have been recorded on the pages of history, who wanted to serve God more than John Wesley. His extensive missionary work among the America Indians, his studious labor in the scriptures; his methodical discipline in personal prayer; his sense of corporate worship revealed a burning desire to serve and love God, but without Saving Faith.

What was true of Wesley before his Aldersgate experience is true of masses who go through our church doors each week. Their spiritual activities are commendable; their charitable hearts are manifesting worthy benevolence, but still the average churchgoer knows nothing of Saving Faith that leads him into the Justifying act that transforms his life into becoming a new creature in Christ Jesus.

There is the Biblical Faith that gets "new birth" results, and then there is that common faith that is universal through common grace. But the differences are as great as the differences between heaven and hell. Wesley noted that most people have some kind of faith. He saw the heathen that believed in a spirit world god, but brutally rejected the living God.

Saving Faith stands out from all other faiths, because this Faith reaches the Living God and brings forgiveness to a sin-cursed inner man. The faith the devils express can not do that; even though they believe and tremble; it is not the faith practiced by moral men; it is not the faith of religious people that we see portrayed worldwide; but it is the Faith that makes the unrighteous righteous; it is the faith that takes wasted lives, and turns them completely around to become vessels for the Master's use only.

Preliminary faith, which in reality is a cultivated common grace, which has put a compassion in man that will be great enough to leave their homes, even their native land, and bury themselves in obscurity among the world's needy. But this dedication does not motivate them to plumb the depths of a Faith necessary for genuine salvation. Preliminary faith always plunges them far below their quest for inner peace that is only found in the personal relationship with the Lord Jesus. But they still struggle on, driving harder to attain that personal satisfaction that is so elusive living in the preliminary faith camp.

Saving Faith rises above the cold calculations of reason; or lifeless assent, and human ideas of morality, and even the human benevolence of common Grace. Saving Faith takes us into more, much more, than religion, it ushers us into Life. Christianity is a Life, not a religion. Religion in itself deadens, but Christ Jesus is Life, and without Him giving this Life, there is no Life. Faith to be Faith must move the Savior into action, Justifying action.

GOOD WORKS CANNOT BE SUBSTITUTED FOR SAVING FAITH!

Natural man can get lost in moralistic ideas that religion presents, and completely by-pass the central Truth that salvation is that which changes the disposition of the heart. Jesus emphasized this Truth in these words: "Many will say to me in that day, Lord, Lord, have we not prophesied in thy name? And in thy name cast out devils? And in thy name done many wonderful work? And then, will I profess unto them, I never knew you: depart from me, ye that work iniquity." (Matt. 7:22-23) What a blow to the pit of the stomach! I cried: "oh God search my heart, I don't ever want to hear those words said to me." What is so tragic, there is no indication these dear people felt their undone and lost condition. Surely their lives were living in preliminary faith, and not Saving Faith.

Saving Faith is believing with the whole heart unto salvation. The soul is brought into oneness by the Saving Faith that wills to pursue God in and through Justification. Anything less is a superficial artificial substitute. Man living in preliminary faith can acknowledge all the cardinal doctrines of the church, subscribe to the Bible as the word of God, take his position with orthodoxy, and still remain in spiritual darkness. Isn't that what Jesus is saying in the above scripture? Saving Faith is not merely this assent to the whole gospel, but rather the full reliance upon the atonement of His sacrificial death and the power of His resurrection to transform the natural heart here and now. Here is the source of the living power that unifies God and man.

Wesley sighted how futile faith is that is not Saving Faith in these words: "Behold I gave all my goods to feed the poor; I have labored more abundantly than they all; I have thrown up my friends, reputation, ease and country; I have put my life in my hand, wandering in strange lands; I have given my body to be devoured by the deep; parched up with heat, consumed by toil and weariness, or whatsoever God should please to bring upon me. But does all this...make me acceptable to God? Does all I ever did or can know, say, give, do, or suffer, justify me in his sight? Yea, or the constant use of all the means of grace?...Or that 'I know nothing of myself;' that I am as touching outward, moral righteousness blameless? Or (to come closer yet), the having a rational conviction of all the truths of Christianity? Does all this give me a claim to the holy, heavenly, divine character of a Christian? By no means, if the oracles of God are true, if we are still to abide by the law and the testimony; all these things, though when ennobled by faith in Christ, they are holy and just and good, yet without it are dung and dross, meet only to be purged away by the fire that never shall be quenched." (*Journal*, J. Wesley, Wed. Feb. 1,1738)

Faith in itself (that which is possessed by most natural men), Wesley found was not adequate to give peace to the inner man. It is more than possessing a religion of a duty bound soul, because the soul refuses to be satisfied with anything less than sonship. The bondage of self has no escape apart from Saving Faith.

Without the personal knowledge that all things have become new, man is without direction and is a roving seeker that never finds his way. However, there is an awareness of an inner power failure that comes with self-generating religiosity. Simply doing good, does not make one righteous in God's sight. Saving Faith brings about the "new birth," which empowers motivational change.

Feverishly men labor, as Wesley, to find salvation through rules, discipline, isolation, church obligations, personal sacrifice, exactness in Liturgy, refusing idleness in search of inward holiness. Wesley's rule in life's action was: "when ever you are to do an action, consider how God did or would do the like, and do you imitate His example." (N. Aurnock's edition of Journal I, p. 48) Notice how thorough Wesley's disciplines were, yet they brought no peace, but rather deeper emptiness. He, like so many others, explored the preliminary regions of faith before the actual knowledge arrived when Saving Faith extended to God's throne and claimed his inheritance, purchased by our Lord, on Calvary's hill.

Dr. John Paul explains Saving Faith this way: "Faith means the acceptance of evidence. If one is intelligent and normal he will believe a statement when sufficient proof is furnished. This natural faith accepts all the rudiments of human knowledge, from the multiplication table to a belief that the earth revolves around the sun.

"All unprejudiced, intelligent students of history, when properly informed accept the wonderful historic facts about the coming of Jesus into this world, the mysterious facts of His Resurrection, after being the victim of capital punishment under Roman law. One may believe all the great fundamental truths of religion and repeat the Apostles' Creed with sincerity; but this variety of faith does not bring an experience and Biblical hope into his heart.

"An over emphasis of ordinances without the true meaning of Saving Faith has some times caused a shallowness in what some have called a revival; where perhaps a number of people with sincere intention have joined some church organization. Saving Faith includes a mental acceptance of gospel truth, an obedience to God's order, and a trust in the Savior. The faith of belief is a good beginning but it takes the faith of trust for one to receive the blessed assurance." (John Paul, *The Herald*)

The apostle Paul was also concerned, that men would not be deceived into allowing the enemy to substitute a preliminary faith for Faith that brings the knowledge of sonship. Writing to the Galatian church, Paul states his inspired position: "Knowing that a man is not justified by the works of the law, but by the faith of Jesus Christ, even we have believed in Jesus Christ, that we might be justified by the faith of Christ, and not by the works of the law: for by the works of the law shall no flesh be justified." (Gal. 2:16)

No man makes a practice of certain disciplines if there is not an element of faith behind what is being done. It can be a very sincere faith and usually is, but always coming short of Saving Faith. Not to understand Saving Faith is to miss the high calling of Christ Jesus, by allowing good works and a preliminary faith to be substituted. An artificial saving faith necessitates a semblance of the equivalent of good works.

HOW AND WHY DOES SAVING FAITH MAKE SUCH A DIFFERENCE?

Why are men not saved without this Faith that has "subdued kingdoms, wrought righteousness, obtained promises, stopped the mouth of lions." (Heb. 11:33)

Saving Faith is never inactive but always operative. It is not produced by what is doing or not doing, but is activated by man's will that wants to do nothing but God's will. Wesley explains Saving Faith in these words: "True faith is not a rational thing, a train of ideas in the head. It is disposition of the heart, generated from the life of the emotions." Here is where many adherents to Christianity have jumped the tracks. In their "do it yourself" Christianity they wish to substitute "ideas in the head" for the genuine Faith that is a forerunner to definite conversion.

Bishop Leslie R. Marston's insight bears the differences in faith. "The Faith by which man finds and follows God is not the barren intellectual faith of the rationalist; nor is it the mystic's feeling, the legalist's works or the ritualist's forms. It is a living Faith that relates the entire being of man to the truth as it is in Christ Jesus."

Saving Faith is not merely a belief, trust or confidence, but all these brought together in actual living Faith In Christ Jesus, which produces holy living and personal piety. If there is anything less than this, it is no more than a religion that has its limits in churchanity; which is rooted in futility and deception.

Philip looked at the current resources of the treasury of the twelve and then at the multitude Jesus wanted to feed and said: "two hundred pennyworth" (John 6:7) would not be enough to cover the cost of such an undertaking. In effect he was saying, Lord, there is no use to start this project, we simply do not have the resources to finish it. Here was a man of faith. He had already left his livelihood and home to follow Jesus. But as so many, if the resources are not on hand there would be no need to expect any type of miracle. To him, limited resources meant the matter was already settled.

What limitations we place on God by what we call faith! Real Faith starts where human resources end. Without an operative faith, it is quite natural to measure God in the light of human resources and capacity. Those who have not gone beyond natural man's faith will easily stop at the present resource level.

Professor John Lawson points out the necessity of faith operating through Saving Faith: "Here is a witness to an actual and objective saving work of Divine Grace, performed in history, written in Scripture, and interpreted in the long experience of the church. Yet it is not by itself enough reverently and thoughtfully to accept this 'train of ideas.' By the inward operation of the Holy Spirit, through the means of grace, the faith must come home, also with power to the secret inward man's heart and the imaginations. To employ an old-fashioned term, Saving Faith is experiential. It is objective, but not barely objective and academic. It is personal, imaginative, and charged with healthy emotion, but not purely subjective. It is the actual outward, and the rational brought home to the heart by the working of the Spirit."

Our God always gives overwhelming proof to a seeking mind that will approach Him without prejudice. Look at the Universe, nothing but an Infinite mind could conceive its galaxies, their orbs, hang them in endless space, regulate their impact on human habitation, supply the necessary resources to sustain life. Who but the Infinite God could create the imponderable phenomenon of the human body's makeup! Who but the

Infinite God could allow His humanity to be drained of life, placed in an empty tomb, guarded by soldiers, and on the third day, as predicted, came out of that tomb, assented into heaven in the presence of a great host whose gaze followed Him as far as their sight would allow. Who but an Infinite God can change a corrupt inner life into the pure redeemed life! This is only a minute picture of the insurmountable evidence that surrounds us, yes, confronts us.

But faith in these facts is not enough to bring the peace of God into the soul. Augustine who recognized the will was the center of Saving Faith made this comment: "he that made us without ourselves, will not save us without ourselves." Saving Faith is the springboard the will has activated in genuine repentance, which can move on quickly to God's justifying act by claiming what was done on Calvary to make this glorious act possible.

Such was the occasion of the prison warden. He held a respectable and responsible position. Many prisoners went through his prison, some notorious and others of the common thug variety. But on this day, he receives two unusual prisoners brought to him for scourging, thrust into the inner prison, and placed in chains. His orders were carried out in his routine way. There was something about these prisoners that was different. They did not curse him for unjustified beating, nor did they shout for revenge.

He left them with bleeding backs, and went about his usual duties. Suddenly there was a song filling the air, coming from the inner dungeon, and then there was a prayer of praise, now unbelievable rejoicing. Suddenly the ground began to roll, rock and shake, the prison walls were crumbling; prisoners were loose running for safety; fear and panic seized the whole area.

The jailer's fears told him to run for his life, but he couldn't. Rome would hunt for him, and he would pay with his life if any of these prisoners escaped. His life depended upon the security of the prisoners. When the dust cleaned, imagine his surprise to find all the prisoners, released from their stocks and chains, standing there.

By now, the message of these two mysterious strangers had reached the jailer's hardened heart. He realized the presence of the Supernatural. From his guilty, sinful heart comes the cry: "Sirs, what must I do to be saved?"

How quickly the jailer had passed through the steps of his personal salvation! It can come just that instantaneously to you. On the other hand, there may be a time element in between each step. Some question every component the Holy Spirit presents; the personal will can battle with The Holy Spirit. Satan will not give up easily. He will place every argument in the book, as to why, each step should not be taken.

Saving Faith must have the ingredients of the simple childlike faith. There is always humility, brokenness, utter surrender and a willingness to be obedient regardless of the cost.

F. B. Sleeper shares this experience from his life that reveals the simplicity of faith that can change and transform the inner being. He says: "The other morning I stood in the stairway of our basement. My little girl was up in the kitchen, and the stairway was dark. I could see her but she could not see me. I said, Darling jump down, and I will catch you. She answered, 'Papa, it is dark down there; I can't see you.' I know it's dark, darling, but I can see you. Jump! Come on! 'But I'm afraid I'll fall and get hurt.' Oh, then you don't trust your Daddy? 'Yes, I do!' How much do you trust me? Do you trust me enough to jump? 'Yes I do.' Come on then. She made a spring and, of course, she landed in my arms. I would not have thought of having her do that if I did not know that I could catch her safely and with out harm."

Saving Faith springs into the arms of the Savior with the full confidence He will do what He has already promised. This is God's Word, which cannot be broken. All of life and eternity rests upon His promises. Saving Faith refuses to believe anything less.

WE CHOOSE WHAT FAITH BY WHICH WE LIVE!

The Scripture gives what genuine Faith is: "faith is the substance of things hoped for, the evidences of things not seen." (Heb. 11:1) Faith, that invisible substance on which a man builds his foundation, on which his soul shall stand for time and eternity. Faith can be built upon sinking sand, or upon the solid rock, Christ Jesus. Each one of us will decide the faith that will guide our lives into the future.

Saving Faith has the substance that demands the soul to surrender utterly, bringing about the disposition of an obedient heart based on the condition of God's Word. While preliminary faith that all humanity possesses, wanders about seeking some foundation of his own making to satisfy himself. Thus, his faith cannot take him any higher than himself. Saving Faith takes the soul beyond himself, resting on our Holy God's bedrock promises.

There must be some way to illustrate the two types of faith which are as far apart as the North and South poles. The following hypothetical case may be crude, but if closely followed will show the marked differences between preliminary faith and Saving Faith.

A man has a malignancy and knows of no cure. Hopelessly, he waits for the grim reaper to knock on his door. The daily paper is brought to his room. A headline catches his eye. This Doctor assures the world, his method of operating will cure the kind of malignancy he has. The article gives the testimony of a number who have been healed. His dying soul is stirred. What news! Hope wells up within him. He rereads the witness of those who had this ill-fated disease. He finds himself saying: "it must be true."

The account he has read has convinced him there is healing available. Despair and doubt are disappearing. But just reading about it, does not cure his disease, even though he is exhibiting a faith that assures him it is true.

It is at this point of faith where multitudes live and die, while still believing this is the faith that makes them Christian. They read the Bible and wholeheartedly believe it to true, knowing it has stood the test of time when higher criticism has sought to wipe its Truth from the face of the earth. Voltaire was one of these infidels that was going to destroy the Bible and make fools out of all that dared to believe its validity. Twenty five years after Voltaire died, his home was purchased by the Geneva Bible Society and became a Bible storage building, and his printing press was used to print an entire edition of the Bible. The Bible testifies that God can and will deliver man from his deadly sin. Multitudes of witnesses have affirmed and declared, by personal experience this does and did happen in their lives. The problem is millions say they believe, even as the man reading the newspaper article, but they are still sin sick. This malignancy must be cured if they are to be saved from eternal death.

Let us take this a step further, as he calls his wife, and has her read the article to see what she thinks. Upon conferring, they decide this is worth investigating. The call is made to the Doctor's office to set up an appointment as soon as possible. Even with this kind of interest, action, and faith, the man still has his disease. So it is with the sin sick soul. He can make an appointment with the Pastor and show great concern, but he still has the sin sickness.

Real faith is shown when he makes the effort to go the Doctor's office. The Doctor's words are encouraging. If he operates now, life can be spared. The man can believe every word the Doctor says, but he still has his disease. Here again, is where many people's faith is. They believe the gospel, but their faith stops, and is inadequate for the sin that is eating them up on the inside. His faith is still preliminary, even though he is reading the Bible and believing every word of it; counseling with the Pastor, and continually telling the Lord how mean and low he has been. He may be weeping tears over the heartache he has caused others. He holds the terror death has over him.

The Doctor now suggests that he will make arrangements for him to enter the hospital. Whoa! Is he willing to go that far? Is his faith adequate for him to obey? With much hesitation, he checks himself into the hospital. He watches the doctors and nurses administer healing to others. The environment of healing is all about him, but he still has his disease.

Let us now parallel this with the spiritual life. Our churches have any number who read their Bibles, pray and attend the services of the church regularly. It is hard to imagine anyone doing these things consistently and not have faith in some measure. However, this daily and weekly effort in itself does not remove the sin problem from the struggling soul. Some have faithfully done these things for years, but still find they are slaves to their passions and fears.

Our sin sick patient is about to be asked to take another step in preliminary faith. His Doctor walks into the room and notifies him he is scheduled for an operation at 7:00 A.M. Suddenly it hits him. This fellow is going to cut on him. This is the real thing. Does he really believe that this Doctor can do what he said he could do? Is he willing to place his life in his hands? What IF his scalpel slips and cuts a vital organ. What IF goes round and round and fear and even terror can mount. Does he want healing that much that he is willing to trust his very life in that man's hands? Faith is pushing him on to complete trust.

Pain and healing seem to go together, neither is easy. Many are in hell today, because they backed away from the Master's surgical knife. They had hoped healing and health would come without surrendering pride and its fellow confidants to the Master's cure. No other remedy will suffice.

This man refused to waver. He could not see any other hope. Now he stands at the crossroads between preliminary faith and Saving Faith. He must chose. Saving Faith means casting EVERYTHING upon the one who has promised to remove the sin disease. Preliminary faith says, stop here, everything is so uncertain, the future is unknown. However, if he makes this decision to reject this means of healing, it will mean certain death. His life is lying in the balance.

Circumstances and time are forcing a decision. He dares not toy with his life. The surgery cart has a screech all its own. It is coming for him. Fear would demand that he reconsider Faith reassures, and urges him to crawl on the cart.

He arrives at the entrance of the operating room, and he can call the whole thing off. But here, his doctor meets him and gives an encouraging touch. But as he lies there, there is a deep realization that the environment of the operating room itself will not deliver him from his disease.

Some dear people have gone as far as the operating room spiritually but still bound in their sins and self-will. They feel that this is far enough, to go the next step is radical, even some feel a fanatical step, going overboard on this religious business. They have never allowed themselves to pass from preliminary faith, to Saving Faith. Healing only comes to the sin diseased soul when all is surrendered to the Master Surgeon, and He goes inside and removes the sins that so easily beset, making all things new. There is no pulling back, or shrinking from the uncertainty of the future. He wants healing more than anything else in life.

It is at this point, Saving Faith kicks into high gear. His struggles cease and he says, I'm in your hands doctor. You know my need and I believe you can meet that need. He submits, to the hurt, the pain, the future, believing this is the only way he can be cured.

What else can be said to the sin sick soul? Saving faith is the hope to those who seek deliverance from the inner corrupt life. Our God is bound by His eternal word to honor such faith that willing gives life and soul. His word speaks so clearly: "Him that cometh to me I will in no wise cast out." (John 6:37)

C. H. Spurgeon asks this question: "Is there any instance of our Lord's casting out a coming one? If there be so, we would like to know about it; but there has been none, and there never will be. Among the lost souls in hell there is not one that can say, 'I went to Jesus, and He refused me.' It is not possible that you or I should be the first to whom Jesus shall break his word. Let us not entertain so dark a suspicion. . .

"This man receiveth sinners, but he repulses none. We come to him in weakness and sin, with trembling faith, and small knowledge, and slender hope; but he does not cast us out. We come by prayer, and that prayer broken; with confession, and confession faulty; with praise, and that praise far short of his merits; but yet he receives us. We come diseased, polluted, worn out, and worthless; but he doth in no wise cast us out."

Quickly this soul passes to the next step, which is Justification.

CHAPTER VI

JUSTIFICATION
What does it mean to be justified?

The result of Saving Faith is immediate. Whenever the conditions are met, there is no delay from moving on. Any interruption is the result of disobedience. Obedience brings instantaneous reward. Paul said it this way: "Therefore being justified by faith, we have peace with God through our Lord Jesus Christ." (Rom. 5:1)

Our Justification is the direct product of Saving Faith that is rooted and grounded in honest obedience and genuine repentance. The moment Saving Faith trusts the Savior for salvation, that quick God acts and sins are forgiven. Justification is being made right in God's sight. It is not bound to creeds, color or social background. Paul reminds the Roman Christians that "by the obedience of one," (Rom. 5:19) all mankind can be justified. He was "obedient unto death." (Phil. 2:8) By obedience he gave, through obedience we have. It is at this point all major denominations agree. Luther, Calvin, Wesley, and other orthodox faiths have made Justification by Faith a Cardinal Doctrine.

Justification is the direct act of God, not by degrees, but instantaneous. Wesley suggests this act takes place "in the twinkling of an eye." All who experience this "new birth" are at that instant free and forgiven of the acts of sins against God. Thus, transformed from a sinner into a saint.

Saving Faith has brought the will to the point of complete surrender so our God actually works righteousness in man and through him. It can be said in a moment, we are justified, acquitted, forgiven, and pronounced guiltless by meeting our Lord's conditions, completely and wholly.

No one can have this miracle happen and not know he has been made right in the sight of God. His knowledge is certain, because he has personally experienced this inward transformation. Such an experience does not find it difficult to understand that at the heart of all God's planning, His aim is to rescue man from his lost and sinful condition.

Justification is defined by Bishop Bull as "acquitting" or "pronouncing guiltless, and therefore, necessarily signifies to acquit an accused person and decree him free from accusation." (Bull, *Harmonica Apostolic*, p. 6 & 7)

George Whitefield explains Justification to be, "so acquitted in the sight of God as to be looked on as though we never had offended Him at all." (Geo. Whitefield, *Works*, Vol. VI, p. 216)

John Wesley understood Justification to be, "as pardon, forgiveness and acceptance by our Lord. When once pardoned, he is immediately adopted into the family of God, and accepted as a son. This union is only possible through Saving Faith." Mr. Wesley wrote in May 1766: "I believe Justification by faith alone as much as I believe there is the God. I declared this in a sermon preached before the University of Oxford, eight-and-twenty years ago. I declared it to all the world eighteen years ago, in a sermon written expressly on the subject. I have never varied from it, no, not a hair's breath, from 1738 to this day." (Wesley Journal, p. 81)

God's mercy will never cease to amaze those who claim His eternal promises. It is not in the heart of God for Him to withhold His Goodness from the repentant no matter how heinous his sins. That one that deserves grievous punishment and ultimate hell, now stands ready to be justified. Not because of any merit whatsoever on man's part, but solely through the merit of Jesus the Savior of all who come unto Him.

Justification source is in the endless infinite Grace of God that pours through Christ Jesus. Paul reminds the Roman church that their foundation is: "Being justified freely by His Grace through the redemption that is in Christ Jesus; whom God hath set forth to be a propitiation through faith in His blood, to declare His righteousness for the remission of sins that are past, through the forbearance of God." (Rom. 3:24-25)

The justifying message is a stream flowing through all Paul's letters. Titus 3:7 stresses the message: "That being justified by his grace, we should be made heirs according to the hope of eternal life."

By the justifying Grace of God, man starts his heavenly journey. Physical birth begins life on this planet. No human being is on this earth except by being born physically. So, it is with Spiritual life. As Jesus said to Nicodemus: "ye must be born again." There is no other way to get into the kingdom of heaven. "He that seeks to climb up some other way, the same is a thief and robber." The Christian life can only start at the point of Justification, without which there is no salvation.

Justification opens the Spiritual eyes, enlightens the understanding and shatters the darkness that once engulfed the soul. What glorious light has dawned, "And the darkness comprehended it not." The stony heart has been broken, whereby "the seed can fall upon good ground" to yield its godly fruit.

Man's motivation center finds a new direction from self-glory to Christ glorying. The ear is opened, the mind is activated with Spiritual comprehension in that gives new insight. The inner being cries out for more of God, the heart has captured His passion; the soul embraces His words: "go and sin more. . .come and follow me."

For the first time life has meaning, filled with purpose and zest; captivated with glory.

JUSTIFICATION UNDERSTOOD AND EXPERIENCED.

Paul reminds the Corinthians: ". . .but ye are washed, but ye are sanctified, but ye are justified in the of the Lord Jesus, and by the Spirit of our God." (1 Cor. 6:11)

A great host of good people never arrive at the place where they know their sins are forgiven through God's Justifying act. They are disturbed, or have settled into an attitude that this the best I can do, and must conclude this is the maximum my religion can give me. This unhappy situation adds more confusion to the spiritual frustration already awakened during those searching times. But so many just keep on running those spiritual circles, ever seeking and never finding.

Here is where frightening inner emptiness compels the spiritual unrest to seek something deeper, (like Sanctification) when actually they have never been Justified. There is no way you can climb salvation's steps by missing steps. It is necessary to come God's way. God is the God of order. Those who refuse to pay that price will seek wild fire religion or some cult to attempt to satisfy the inner hunger. Or become utterly defeated and give up.

John Wesley was an example of one who found in his early life the rising and falling in one spiritual dilemma after another. His holy habits, missionary work, church membership, scholarship, home back ground still left him without God's peace, which is the only one that can give inward peace. He had by-passed the Justification step. There is no way to win when that is done.

There is a plague in our churches that has robbed church-goers of their hope of salvation by replacing personal justification with average church morality. The Jews believed salvation was keeping the law. This brought about an open clash between our Lord and the temple leadership, which eventually climaxed at Calvary. The disciples' ministries were in constant conflict which cost their lives, (except one), and the stream of martyr's blood is flowing through history. Because of this lack of understanding, they shed innocent blood and shut the door to their personal salvation.

Dr. Robert G. Lee suggests that: "Multitudes of church members today are being offered a chunk of cloud bank buttered with the night wind instead of Christianity's vital, life giving bread. There is no gospel if the atoning blood of Christ is omitted, if the virgin birth is denied, if Christ's resurrection is eliminated, if justification by faith is not preached."

There is a peace that passeth all understanding for every seeking soul. Possibly modern man living in today's turmoil believes such possibilities as only pious legends, but for the heart that reaches out in saving faith, he can experience this truth for himself.

The justifying act removes the burden of guilt and despair. The heart takes up a new song, a joy that does not subside in the midst of adverse circumstances. The soul has a discernment that can evaluate temptation in the light of God. The resurrection that has taken place in the inner man brings a fullness and richness that dispenses fear and doubt.

Once sin is removed, the inner life suddenly finds itself flooded with the immeasurable love stream of God. This quickening releases an undivided devotion and praise to the Savior. Divine illumination explodes with sacred fire, realizes the saturation of Spiritual liberty.

There is a freedom that consummates the need of man's soul. The heavy chains weighed with guilt pushed sanity to the edge, justifying Grace brings glorious emancipation; a knowledge that understands perfectly what Wesley meant when he said now he was "an altogether Christian." The whole being is now engrossed with a totally new aspirations and desires. There is but one purpose for the justified man, to completely fulfill his Lord's every wish and will for his life.

For the first time, the justified man experiences Spiritual health. Fair summer religion is replaced with a living faith that transcends the old haunting fears. The failure of personal morality has given way to the all conquering victory over willful sin. Old laborious duties become new delights.

Through the power that came into Wesley's life on May 24, 1738, the whole course of the British Empire felt the impact, and history was changed. The barriers of the oceans themselves were not great enough to retain the power released. Wesley's justifying experience leaped across the Atlantic, and ignited the fires of the Great Awakening and the frontier revivals.

An English lad of 15 started to his church one stormy Sunday in January 1850. The storm turned him into Primitive Methodist Chapel on Artillery Street. The regular minister did not come, but a layman stepped to the pulpit to take charge. (Little do we realize the depth and the importance of each service.) This 15-year-old six years later tells what happened.

"Six years ago today, as near as possible at this very hour of the day, I was in the gall of bitterness and in the bonds of iniquity, but had yet by divine grace been led to feel the bitterness of that bondage and to cry out by reason of the soreness of its slavery. Seeking rest and finding none, I stepped within the house of God and sat there afraid to look upward lest I should be utterly cut off and lest his fierce wrath should consume me. The minister rose in his pulpit, and, as I have done this morning, read this text, "Look unto me, and be ye saved, all the end of the earth: for I am God, and there is none else." (Isa. 45:22)

"I looked that moment. The grace of faith was vouchsafed to me in the self-same instant, and now I think I can say with truth –
'Were sense by faith, I saw the stream,
Thy flowing wounds supply,
Redeeming love has been my theme,
And shall be till I die!" (Wm. Cowper)

It was that Justifying experience that produced that miraculous change that turned his life completely around. The potential was liberated to be used of God to reach multitudes, and point them to the Cross.

JUSTIFICATION – FREE TO ALL!

The word "whosoever" presented in the Bible looms tall and sufficient for every soul. Hope rises for all mankind when these marvelous words hit the mind – "For God so loved the world, that he gave his only begotten Son, that WHOSOEVER believeth in him should not perish, but have everlasting life," The door is open to "whosoever" will come with a surrendered will.

There is no way that God will include a chosen few to be Justified, and exclude others, and retain His attribute of Justice. It would be condemning arbitrarily the excluded without giving them a choice. The Bible is deluged with the responsibility for accountability. If there is no accountability, how can God judge with any Justice? Man is on trial now, but how can guilt be put on trial if guilt has no way to be acquitted. The trial is fixed and there isn't anything the lost can do about it. How unjust that kind of theology is!

It is only proper to present the two contested views on God's Grace at this point. Dr. William Cannon considers the division in his book – *The Theology of John Wesley*: "The Calvinistic conception of grace, therefore, rests squarely on the conviction of the absolute sovereignty of God. God orders completely everything that he has created; and all events of the universe, from the highest to the lowest, are according to his will. Nothing happens by accident or by any power not itself the instrument of the divine choice. Saving grace is applied only where God chooses to apply it; it is always effective, irresistible, and complete." (Does not this make God the culprit that caused Adam to sin?)

"The Wesleyan conception of the nature of the operation of God's grace is as far removed from the Calvinistic conception as the east is from the west. Saving grace is not restricted; it is not particular; it does not rest on the prior principle of election or predestination. 'How freely does God love the world! While we were " dead in sin," God "spared not his own Son,' but delivered him up for us all.' And how freely with him does he 'give us all things!' Verily 'free grace' is all in all! p. 59 Yes, and Wesley goes on to write in a sermon which Tyerman says," in some respects was the most important sermon that he ever insured' p. 60 that the grace or love of God, whence cometh our salvation, is 'free in all, and free for all.' p. 61 To be sure, it is free in all in the sense that it is given without price, that it does not demand anything of us before it is bestowed, and that it flows from the free mercy of God. p. 62 Here Wesley is in fundamental agreement with the thought of Calvin and of Whitefield. But not the change. Grace is free for all as well as free in all. It is not free only for those whom God has ordained to life, but it is like the air we breathe or like the wind that blows in our faces." (Wm. Cannon, *The Theology of John Wesley*, p. 93)

Why would our God go to such an extent to bring about the availability of justifying Grace for man? God's personality and nature is to love and to be loved. It is also displayed in mankind, as the Father created this same attribute in man. But love is a two-way street. It is not love in its completeness, until love is returned to the lover.

Another asks, is man worth what it cost God to justify him? Jesus answers the question when he reminded us that as far as God is concerned, one soul is worth more than the whole world. "Ye are not your own, but ye are bought with a price." How else can we evaluate His love, that He would give Himself as the only sacrifice acceptable. The songwriter put it this way, "Love so amazing, so divine."

Dr. Cannon asks the question: "Why, we ask, is man pardoned? What prompts God to free him from guilt? If to justify does not mean to purify – if to pronounce guiltless does not mean to cleanse from actual sin – then it follows that one of two things must be the case: either God's justifying grace does not concern itself in the least with man's moral state but rather operates arbitrarily, freeing him from the punishment and yet leaving him in the practice of his sins; or else God's justifying grace does concern itself exclusively with man's moral state and operates according to moral law, coming as a consequence of, not as a means to, righteousness, freeing a man from punishment only when that man himself is actually free from sin." (Wm. Cannon, *The Theology of John Wesley*, p. 37)

Just because man is justified, does not mean he has lost his accountability. Does it not make man more accountable, simply because now he has more light? Man's probation does not end with Justification. The same Grace that saved, is able to keep man pure and free from sin.

This justifying state must be fruitful. There is no way to obtain this spiritual state before personal Justification, but after this glorious experience, the daily life will give clear evidence, that Godly fruit is being produced.

I read of a school teacher who felt money was the most important thing in life. In fact, the teacher's salary, was not enough to satisfy his greedy thirst, so he got an additional job. Then, something wonderful happened, that changed his entire motivation. God heard his sinner's cry, and did that miracle of miracle, forgiving his sins and giving a new heart. Now, all things became new, he quit his extra job so he would have time to serve the Lord.

THE DIFFERENCES BETWEEN IMPUTED RIGHTEOUSNESS AND IMPARTED RIGHTEOUSNESS.

When the soul is justified, man receives imputed righteousness, for he has none of his own. The Father only accept His righteousness. But too often, the introspective work of the Holy Spirit that imparts righteousness, and makes man righteous and pure within is overlooked. Imputed righteousness is a surrounding righteousness, while imparted righteousness is implanted by the Holy Spirit into a completely cleansed heart, filled with the Holy Spirit, giving victory over sin. Imputed righteousness is the legal transaction that makes us right in the sight of God. We could not appease God with anything but Christ's righteousness. Imputed righteousness leaves us only being "in Christ." But the Bible teaches us that Christ can also be "in us." Making us responsible to act and live like Him.

Some are guilty of using imputed righteousness as a cloak for personal sinning, and as an escape from the responsibility God's light gives the justified man on his inbred sin. Christ did not come to save us in our sin, or with our sins, but He came to deliver us from our sins. "Shall we continue in sin, that Grace may abound? God forbid! How shall we that are dead to (the) sin, live any longer therein?" (Rom. 6:1-2) If this is true, and it is, then our God must also have made a provision to impart righteousness so man can have imparted righteousness to obey His commandments, and love Him with the whole heart. This righteousness must be adequate to give victory over inbred sin if the atonement is sufficient for ALL sin, and it is. This will be dealt with more fully in Sanctification's step.

The word "imputed" means something that is credited to your account. While imparted righteousness means we are partakers of His righteousness by actually possessing His imparted righteousness, "Christ IN you, the hope of glory."

Imputed Righteousness conveys the conception that the Atonement does not change the nature of sin and devastation carnality has on man; thus, saving man in his sins, rather than from his sins. Man's nature relates only to the sins he has committed and those he will continue to commit. Sin is shorn of its power and can no longer damn the soul or separate the individual from God, even though he continues to commit the most foul of sins.

Why, because of Christ's Imputed Righteousness, even though sin is active in his daily life. The claim is, sin has lost its power, thus, made possible by Christ's Imputed righteousness. Any willful sin is already covered. Past, present, and all future sins are charged to Christ's account, automatically covering the sins believers commit and will commit. Sin is charged to Christ's account, and His Righteousness is charged to our account, even if an immoral life is continued. No matter how ungodly the life is lived after accepting Christ, the Atonement covers all the willful daily sins of the believer's sins so the Father does not see them.

This type of Theology claims man is pure because Christ is pure, regardless of how impurely he lives. In other words, the Atonement is limited, because there is no freedom from sin so man can live a pure and holy life. In this Theology there is no way man can be delivered from his carnality, that evil nature incarnated at birth.

John Fletcher wrote of John Wesley: "with thee I gladly would both live and die." Both took a stand against the legalized concept of a sinning religion in the daily life of a believer. Antinomianism is a legal standing without an inward state of purity, resting in the work of God rather than in God Himself. Taking the position, I am holy because God is holy; I never sinned because Christ never sinned. It shifts the meritorious cause of Justification from the death of Christ to the life of Christ. Thus, making His death wholly unnecessary, relying totally on Imputed Righteousness, that denies the entitlement of Imparted Righteousness that cannot be satisfied with anything less than personal holiness within.

This philosophy entertained hostile thought towards the law of Moses, leading to a tendency to immoral practice and teaching. In its inception, even harlotry was not sinful to the Spiritual man; suggesting nothing is sin except if man believes it to be so, destroying the moral law of the Old Testament. Making Christians free from the law of Moses, not subject to any law other than the subjective impulse that could change one's mind, leaving the empirical individual as the interpreter of the Holy Spirit.

This led many as Agricola, to fear "works" as the means to salvation leading him to argue against the moral law. Suggesting that man is saved by faith alone, without regard to his moral character, even after his conversion. Calvin argued, "if a man was elected and predestined to salvation, no power in heaven or on earth could prevent it; no matter what the moral conduct of a man might be, his salvation was sure if he was one of the elect; the wicked actions of such a man were not sinful, and he would have no occasion to confess his sins, or to break them off by repentance."

By this theological position, it leaves man without accountability. Especially, if predestination is interwoven, man is not responsible before or after conversion. The elect's obligation for his moral life, and accountability to his God was mere relativism.

The anarchism of the Anabaptists was an offshoot of this idea of resisting the law. They demanded to be free from any and all laws. Anarchism means the perfectly unfettered self-government of the individual, without the interference from any external law. The law was considered enslavement and no man should be in such bondage. They felt this freedom would give man the perfect harmony needed for unlimited sweeping liberty to explore man's immeasurable powers. Now man could see the wonders of sharing so that all could advance, which would include

Collectivism and Socialism. The natural evolution would be an integrated productivity that would lead to the common good of the whole. This would be the natural outcome of the free life, where there would not be anything impeding each person's possibilities. Their basis logic was the will of each is the will of God. Man must be his own governor. This would create progress by evolution, rather than revolution. Much of their thinking was pantheism, because they made God a part of the universe and could not separate God and the universe, leaving man on his own. Modern thought has absorbed much of this philosophy.

Justification must include accountability not only to God but others that we can lead or mislead. It does not leave us to act on our own. He who paid the price to justify the believer, also claims rights to his created, and refuses to allow His treasured creation to wallow in willful sin. God hates sin and went to the extreme extent to save man from its deadly clutches, and will cut off those who rebel against His word, as fruitless branches that reject the vine.

Some think that to be "justified" is simply to be forgiven. But the word represents something greater still. The justified man, and he is, is every man who has come to God in Christ, is not only forgiven, but regarded in God's sight as though he had never sinned. He is a man against whom God has no charge while he walks in the light of holy obedience. He can, however, violate his probation and transgress, but not without guilt and accountability to God's justice.

This is illustrated by James Gray in the case of the French military officer, Captain Dreyfus. You remember that he was charged with selling French military secrets to the German army and was court-martialed for it. Because he was a Jew his hearing was utterly unfair, and in the face of evidence he was accounted guilty, and banished to Devil's Island. But there were friends who kept agitating for a second trial, and when this was brought about, again in the face of the evidence, he was found guilty. Now, however, the President of France, to save the face of the nation, pardoned him. Captain Dreyfus is free. He may go where he pleases, and do what he likes.

But he is not satisfied with pardon; nor his friends, nor a large portion of France. The whole world indeed, has awakened to the unfairness of the judgment, and cried out for another trial that the pardoned man might be justified. The third trial is granted and at last Captain Dreyfus is justified of the crime. He is not pardoned now, but something different and something better. He is now regarded in the eyes of France and of the world as one who never committed the crime.

There are only two ways in which a man can be justified of a crime. One is on the merits of being innocent; the other on the ground of paying the penalty for it, or someone else paying the penalty. Captain Dreyfus was justified on the fact of innocence, for he was innocent. You and I cannot be justified on the argument that we are innocent of sin, for we are guilty. But we who have accepted by Christ Jesus through Saving Faith are justified on the rationale that another has paid the penalty of our sin, in every way, not in and of ourselves, but in the person of our substitute, who died, "the just for the unjust, that He might bring us to God."

JUSTIFICATION RESULTS IN RECONCILIATION!

By God's Justification act, lost man is now reconciled back to God through our Lord. There is no reconciliation until the act of removing man's sin is done. This could not be done without the holy God becoming the scapegoat. With the sins of all generations upon Him, He casts them as far as the east is from the west, for all who repent and believe unto salvation. His blood shed as a sacrifice, an offering, the innocent for the guilty.

Dr. Harold Greenlee, a Greek scholar says: "Reconciliation with God means that we must become "other" than what we are by nature. Yet it is not merely "other". First, it means "thoroughly other" than what we were. Secondly, this "otherness" is a transformation which God accomplishes, through Christ, in order to make us fit for His presence. It therefore means exchanging our sinfulness for a heart, life, and character which reflect His holiness and purity." (*The Herald*, 1-9-63)

Paul in 2 Corinthians 5:17-21 describes this Spiritual transformation in these words: "Therefore if any man be in Christ, he is a new creature: old things are passed away; behold, all things are become new. And all things are of God, who hath reconciled us to himself by Jesus Christ, and hath given to us the ministry of reconciliation; to wit, that God was in Christ, reconciling the world unto himself, not imputing their trespasses unto them; and hath committed unto us the word of reconciliation. Now then we are ambassadors for Christ, as though God did beseech you by us: we pray you in Christ's stead, be ye reconciled to God. For He hath made Him to be sin for us, who knew no sin; that we might be made the righteousness of God in Him."

Monument of this reconciliation are every where. They may not be the majority, but wherever they are they stand out like a lighted city in the dead of night on a lonely hillside.

Let Paton's witness to the transforming Grace be heard and felt: "After three years of incredible discouragements and fantastic perils, Paton baptized his first converts on the South Sea island of Aniwa. The tide turned, and before long almost the entire population of Aniwa, a race of lying, treacherous, and blood-thirsty cannibals, hateful and hating one another, had been converted into honest, peaceful, loving, and forgiving Christians. The miracle of Fije (where a hundred thousand ferocious cannibals were converted to 'the new religion of peace and love' (within forty years) was repeated."

In his autobiography, Paton told the story of the first communion service celebrated on Aniwa "since the island was heaved out of its moral depth!" ..."For three years we had toiled and prayed and taught for this. At the moment when I put the bread and wine into those dark hands, once stained with the blood of cannibalism, now stretched out to receive and partake the emblems and seals of the Redeemer's love, I had a foretaste of the joy of glory that well-nigh broke my heart to pieces. I shall never taste a deeper bliss till I gaze on the glorified face of Jesus Himself."

When a soul is justified (made right in the sight of God), he possesses a new life. May I say, a completely changed life, separated from willful sin, as a regenerated soul.

CHAPTER VII

REGENERATION
When does this walk start and what does it reveal?

Justification, the act of God that makes the sinner right in God's sight, and imparts His peace in the inner being, has brought new life to the seeker. This new life is called Regeneration. There is therefore no commendation, no willful estrangement between the Justified soul and his Maker. Premeditated sin has been forsaken, holy obedience has taken its place. Now God and man walk together. What glorious reality! The change that takes place will be energized by God's power with amazing results. Paul wrote this to the Corinthians: "therefore if any man be in Christ, he is a new creature, old things pass away; behold, all things become new." (2 Cor. 5:17) A reality only the Redeemed know.

Wesley longed for this inward power that changes life. He encountered Thomas á Kempis' book, The Christian Pattern, that encouraged him to seek inward religion. William Cannon relates this revelation in these words: "Wesley attributed the discovery of 'The Christian Pattern' to the providence of God, for through its pages the nature and extent of inward religion now appeared to him in a stronger light than ever before. He saw for the first time that true religion must be seated in the heart and that God's laws must extend to a man's thoughts as well as to his words and actions. He knew now that Thomas á Kempis, that "person of great piety and devotion," meant in regard to both sincerity and purity; and from his work he learned "that 'simplicity of intention and purity of affection,' one design in all we do, without which he can never ascend to the mount of God." (*The Theology of John Wesley*, p. 56)

Every Justified child of God knows by experience this inward changing power. This type of knowledge can only be known by those who are born into His kingdom. This birth can only happen by an act of God. This is the door to ultimate Truth. Justified man now has certainty (not in the realm that all truth has suddenly blossomed before him), but in the scope of an entrance, that contains endless truth. Now, God and man are walking and communing together, which is the Regenerated life. The Regenerated life allows man to see beyond himself. Life that was small and limited to self-interest suddenly blooms, as if it is being telescoped by the Infinite God, and allowing Him to take the soul into a whole new world. The New Life is linked in an intimacy that only Redeemed man can have with His Creator. Remember, the half has never been told or known. Each day, He reveals a little more of His purpose for me. This always opens up the endless possibility of God working through man.

Bishop Werner gives a forceful illustration of what happens in redeemed man in these words: "In the second World War, a company of American soldiers on Okinawa was approaching a village, a tiny village known as Shimabuku. Thirty years previously a missionary had stopped in that village, made two converts, left a Bible, and then went on to Japan. No Christian had visited this place since then. Now the GI's were moving toward the village that lay directly in the path of their advance. On the edge of it they were met by two men, the two original converts. One of them had become the chief of the village, and the other the teacher. With the aid of the Bible they had Christianized the entire village. They created a life and society in that village based upon the principles of Jesus, and now they came bowing their welcome to the GI's saying, "we are Christians, too." As the soldiers entered the village, they saw homes that were spotlessly clean; they met villagers who were gentle, healthy, and happy. It was overwhelming. One old, tough sergeant said to his commanding officer, "I can't figure it, this kind of people coming out of only a Bible and a couple of old guys who wanted to live like Jesus!" Then he added, "maybe we've been using the wrong kind of weapons to make the world over." (*No Saints Suddenly*, p. 18 & 19)

Shimabuku stood as a testimony to God and man walking together in redemptive companionship. In this new life, Spiritual affections and treasures are changed. Now one desire stands out, to please God only. This innovative resurrected soul seeks unprecedented ways to serve His Master. The heart takes on a fresh zeal, that knows no service too small or great.

Thus, this change of human desires is love motivating that pushes self-centerness aside to make way for the willing cross bearer. This is the core and marrow of the scripture. Nothing penetrates as deeply as God's light, which illuminates all shadows and every nook and cranny of the inner life. The hub of the Spiritual life is focused on a love binding God and man together. The result is an overflow of love for lost humanity.

THE CONFLICT!

This God and man walk will not advance too long before redeemed man becomes aware that there is still something in him that is rebelling against God. It is causing conflict. Self insists to be on the throne, and a saved man knows that God must always be on the heart's throne. As this war increases and victory over this nature becomes less, defeat is inevitable, if God is not sought with all the heart, mind, soul and strength.

What is so disruptive, at times the inner man vents a nasty and mean spirit, anything but Christlike. These shocking experiences leave the man in despair and the conscience fired with guilt. The reconciliation of God and man is put in jeopardy because of the hostility of the old nature still remaining in man, that refuses to surrender to God's whole will. This man is experiencing a spirit that at times is shaking a fist at God, when God says, "do," but is informed by his carnal nature, "I won't." A few weeks after Charles Spurgeon's marvelous conversion, he cried, "my soul seems to lust after the flesh pots of Egypt, and that after eating heavenly manna, help and forgive me, O my Savior." This is the cry of every justified soul after encountering the carnal nature that has surprised the thrilling experience of the new birth. The joy was so full, there was no thought that there could be anything within that could possibly disturb it. But there it is, often donating and forcing unruly and ungodly actions.

The Apostle Paul describes the carnality that the believer is wrestling with in these words: "For that which I do I allow not: for what I would, that I do not; but what I hate, that I do." (Rom. 7:15) All men of genuine faith have found this action coming from within, and breaking the heart time after time. Gairdner found his carnal nature swept by ecstasies and agonies. He became a man of strong emotions so held in control that very few guessed how fierce were the inner storms that tore him apart within. It is the inner storms, the civil war within, that is the constant drag on the soul of the sincere Christian. Instead of the regenerated life being one of constancy, it becomes, all too many times, one of unwilling defeat and despair. This desperate and serious soul may not know the theological terms that are tacked on his raging infernal within, but he KNOWS something is radically wrong. The foundation of his spiritual house is stressed from pillar to stern; devastated with the lack of godly control. Doing what he hates, and knowing what he should not do, is overwhelming, crushing out the spiritual life, which he longs to live in victory.

There are many Biblical terms used to identify this rebellious nature, such as: the "Old man," (Rom. 6:6; Eph. 4:22; Col. 3:9) "the flesh" is found in Rom. 7:14, 25; 8:4, 8, 13; "the carnal mind," Rom. 8:7. Other names are "self", "enmity." No matter what this nature is called, it is the fallen nature received from Adam's race, and if willfully harbored will add up to spiritual defeat. This nature has a personality that refuses to surrender wholly to the Lord God, exerting a self-will that manifests itself at the most inopportune times and that brings reproach and shame on the Savior. There is a bent toward evil that creates a twisted and warped view of complete and entire obedience to the whole will of God.

INVOLUNTARY SIN!

Since the believer is acutely aware that there is an unending battle that is explosive on the spur of the moment; honesty demands a solution. What is so alarming to the believer, he is doing what he doesn't want to do. In fact, he is living in involuntary sin. "For the good that I would, I do not: but the evil which I would not, that I do. Now if I do that I would not it is no more I that do it, but sin that dwelleth in me." (Rom. 7:19-20)

There is willful sin, and there is involuntary sin. Willful sin is when personal will is exerted against God's will. It is a deliberate choice to go contrary to God's will for your life. The individual now becomes a transgressor that has determined to place personal will above God's. When God's will and man's will cross, this is trouble city.

Involuntary sin is sin that is acted out without the will being activated. There is no time to think, like stubbing the toe on the bedpost. The wrathful expelling of unmentionable words spill out before you could think what happened. There was no forethought before the words poured out. But nevertheless, there had to be this rottenness on the inside before it could come out, without deliberate thought or premeditated motivation. Because it was not willful and deeply despised, it cuts profoundly into the conscience, revealing the ugliness of an enemy within. The remorse is so shattering the honest believer could tear the uncontrollable tongue from his mouth. How distasteful is this kind of spirit and action to the justified soul. He prays Charles Wesley's words in the second verse of Love Divine:

"Breathe, O Breathe Thy loving Spirit into every troubled breast!
Let us all in Thee inherit, Let us find the promised rest;
Take away our bent to sinning; Alpha and Omega be;
End of faith, as its beginning, Set our hearts at liberty."

Because repentance has been genuine and justification personal and real, the flame has a burning desire for complete victory over all self and involuntary sin. This conviction can be more burdensome than the penetrating conviction before conversion. Now the spirit is more sensitive, and the conscience is enlightened by being made alive by the justifying act that opened a greater insight into Divine Truth. This changed the whole concept about who his Master is, causing these involuntary out-breaks to be unacceptable and terrifying to the Spiritually discerning soul.

Behavior is not necessarily a desire, but can be an involuntary reaction to an inward condition that is reintroduced time after time without time to evaluate. (Such as, when someone slams the car hood down on your hand.) This carnal nature is a monster that is a law unto itself, and refuses to be governed by God or man. Paul said the carnal nature is enmity against God.

THE DIFFERENCE BETWEEN PHYSICAL LIMITATIONS AND THE CARNAL NATURE!

Too many confuse the carnal nature with physical limitations. John R. Brooks' book *Scriptural Sanctification*, (p. 15) clearly states the difference: "By physical depravity is meant the impairment of the substance of the mind or body, resulting from the fall. This may be called the weakness or disease of our nature from which proceed many errors of judgment and consequent blunders in the outer life, neither of which involves a bias toward evil – a bent toward selfishness and sinfulness – the inclination to what is inconsistent with love to God and man."

While the carnal nature can be cleansed from its self-centeredness, and evil bentness; physical depravity caused by the fall, which includes everything humanly physical will remain in that state of infirmed limitation. The carnal nature is a spiritual condition which the atonement is adequate to cleanse and purify, while our physical makeup is a part of our physical being, impaired in our earthly journey, which only the new resurrected body will eliminate.

The carnal nature makes us aware of wrongful and evil impurities that are within rebelling against God which is condemning, while human infirmities may cause pain but not condemnation. These physical disorders restrict, but merit an awareness of more dependence upon God's Grace. Physical obstructions can be our strength, but carnal impediment will be our downfall. They are different in the fact that one is spiritual and the other is physical.

THE FACT OF INWARD DEPRAVITY IN THE BELIEVER, AND ITS CONSEQUENCES!

Professor William Barclay in his book, *Flesh and Spirit*, describes the regenerated life as: "The flesh is the great enemy of the good life, and of the Christian life. . .In the sarx (flesh), nothing good dwells. . . it is exactly here that we see the difference between soma and sarx, body and flesh. The body can become the instrument of the service and glory of God; the flesh cannot. The body can be purified and even glorified; the flesh must be eliminated and eradicated."

There is no other way to have complete victory in the Christian life. The internal carnal struggle must cease, and wholeness must be the order of every day. This every honest believer knows. The carnal attitudes and the wrong spirit does not and cannot please Him who calls men to be holy as He is holy.

DIFFERENCE BETWEEN MISTAKES AND CARNAL SIN!

Carnal sin is rooted in a polluted nature. Its source is always twisted and bent when it is measured with God's Holiness. Carnal sin always has self-will behind the intention, that is flushed with insidious implications. Its influence produces a continual layer of pride that fosters disdain towards holy living; such contempt lays disgrace at the foot of the cross as its state of grace. This nature clouds and prohibits the perfect will of God working through and in the believer.

Mistakes are the result of wrong judgment, that can have a pure motive. There is no malicious consideration. It is acted upon with clear conscience, which includes the finite limitations of being human. Mistakes cannot be made with evil or prejudice in mind. A mistake is innocent if motive is pure. If motive is not pure, then it ceases to be a mistake and becomes a carnal act.

Temptation is never sinful in itself. Temptation can only become sin when there is a yielding to the sinful appeal. The enticement is more attractive when there is a carnal nature within that already has a bridgehead that is contrary to the whole of God's will. Because man is free to choose, it becomes much easier to choose transgression when there is something on the inside that is sympathetic to ungodliness. The hurt deepens when the Holy Spirit speaks inwardly about the necessity to be wholly yielded to holy living. This knowledge is so definite, it is unmistakably true and refuses to be excused. Temptation will always be a fact that all must continually confront, but the Spirit filled soul has three-fourths of the battle won because there is nothing within that wants what the Devil has to offer. That does not mean that the enemy can not set up an enticing situation. But to one who is utterly and completely sold out to the Lord, when the choice is there, there is nothing as appealing as what the Lord has done, and is doing, in the tempted one's life. Sanctification gives that victory over temptation and sin.

THE DIFFERENCES BETWEEN THE NATURAL DRIVES AND CARNAL NATURE!

The human nature (or possibly it should be said, the natural God given drives that are a part of the human system), are unique, and totally different from the carnal nature. These drives can be sinful if not used within God's guide lines. That can come about when the carnal nature is the instrument used to divert the natural drives into lustful and evil motives.

Because these God given drives are innate, Satan would use them to confuse the difference between an indigenous drive and a carnal drive. The inherent drives are sinless when conducted within God's guidelines, while these same drives can become sinful whenever they step beyond those guidelines. God's Word clearly makes the distinction.

H. A. Baldwin in his book *Holiness and the Human Element* evaluated the difference this way: "While we live in this world we will never be wholly free from physical desires and appetites! In themselves these drives and appetites are legitimate and are not a sign of depravity, but when men fell, their natural appetites become depraved, and will never, in this life, reach such a state that their possessors will not be forced to deny themselves daily – to keep their bodies under control. In other words, while, in the article of holiness, moral depravity is removed, yet physical depravity remains, and a man must deny his inordinate appetites, tastes, desires and preference." (p. 88 & 89)

IS GOD'S PURPOSE FOR FULL SALVATION COMPLETED IN THE DIVINE ACT OF JUSTIFICATION AND MAN'S WALK IN REGENERATION?

Bishop Foster anticipated this question and answered it this way: "Is not the work of God perfect in regeneration? If you mean, is not the soul regenerated? We answer, certainly it is: but if you mean, is it not thereby perfectly holy we must answer, it does not so seem to us. When a soul is regenerated, all the elements of holiness are imparted to it, or the graces are implanted in it, in complete number, and the perfection of these graces is entire sanctification; and hence, we insist that entire sanctification does not take place in regeneration, for the graces are not then perfect." (*Christian Purity*, Bishop R. S. Foster, p. 15 & 16)

Too many professing Christians stop at the seventh chapter of Romans and never reach the eighth chapter and on. The believer's salvation is never full until carnality is removed and there is no condemnation caused by the involuntary sin.

THE TWOFOLD NATURE OF SIN!

The regenerated man knows his sins are forgiven, he can never forget that, but he also is aware that he is two people on the inside. One wants to live a holy life and one wants to let the fleshly desires dictate the lifestyle. Justification has forgiven him of his acts of sin (notice these sins are plural), where his will was willed against the Lord God. The Psalmist prayed, "blot out my transgressions," (plural) but he did not stop there, there was a deeper need, so he cries: "wash me thoroughly from mine iniquity, and cleanse me from my sin." (Ps. 51:2) Notice "my sin" he is now aware that he is accountable for his sin nature, which is singular. His transgressions needed to be forgiven, his iniquity (carnal nature) needed to be cleansed. This reveals the fact that sin is twofold. In order for man to know and experience full salvation, it necessitates two works of Grace, forgiveness and cleansing. When the sin nature is cleansed, condemnation is gone, there is no condemnation to those fully in Christ Jesus. Each experience is a separate act of God.

This understanding makes the regenerated man coincide with the scripture. He knows he has been forgiven, but he is equally aware that his nature has not been cleansed of the sin problem it is causing. It is not the willful acts that are giving him trouble, but it is that carnality that rises up within that brings crushing and devastating defeat. The honest man of God is pulverized by doing what he doesn't want to do, finding himself involuntarily bringing shameful disgrace upon the Master he loves. Anguish and remorse shatters the earnest soul at these distraught times.

All men are born with a bent, twisted nature. In Adam all died by his direct disobedient act against God's will. This violation brought physical death to mankind, but also caused spiritual death to enter the human race.

First, we did not have anything to do with Adam's willful transgression that caused this atrocious conduct. Therefore, we acquire a nature that curses us without our will being involved. We can't ask forgiveness for that which we never willed. We can only ask forgiveness for our personal disobedience. The regenerated life knows this burden of guilt is gone, forgiven.

Secondly, this forgiven soul has an alarm go off within saying there is something remaining that at times fights doing God's will in provocative areas. What is so disturbing? It acts without the will being activated, wrecking havoc with the daily Christian walk There was no awareness of its carnality until the sins were forgiven. This devastating discernment was a startling awakening that became more troubling as the sensitivity of the conscience was kindled by the Holy Spirit.

Since this carnality is bringing a continual reproach upon all that is holy, it becomes a definite issue which cannot be ignored. When the Holy Spirit starts to plumb the soul's depth, things will be uncovered, revealing carnality's ugliness and just how corrupt the polluted nature is. Anything that diminishes the spiritual life must become an immediate issue. Since this is so, the understanding makes us accountable. Now we know! Furthermore, we know the precious Atonement was for all sin, or else we are forced to believe in a LIMITED ATONEMENT. As a result of this knowledge, there is no way we can deny its existence and continue to harbor this contaminated potency that will destroy the holy life. If the Atonement is sufficient for all sin, then the cleansing of this sinister forbidden nature can be purified through the cleansing agency of the Holy Spirit, when the soul is utterly and wholly surrendered to the whole will of God. What deliverance!

Moses recognized the twofold nature of sin. It is very clear in the commandments, he said: "Thou shalt not steal." To steal, you must act. Then he said: "Thou shalt not covet."

Coveting is not a physical act, it is an inward motive. As far as the Lord is concerned, one is just as much forbidden as the other. The act must be forgiven, while the motive must be cleansed to be pure.

It is only while walking in the regenerated life that the believer becomes cognizant of a wick self-centered ego that refuses to be subject to the law of God. To realize that there is a censorious spirit in the honest believer who wants only to please God, will cause endless tears of unrest, and inner turmoil. Sin's carnal bent can never successfully be curbed by self-discipline or human suppression. The carnal nature is an outlaw that stubbornly resists all effort to keep it in restraints. It is the strange and paradoxical self-contradiction of fallen man. It is "enmity against God: for it is not subject to the law of God; neither indeed can be." (Rom. 8:7) This debased nature's capabilities are given in Paul's letter to the Galatian church. (Gal. 5:19-21)

Someone may honestly ask, are you saying that Satan is in the heart of the justified believer, as well as Christ? This can not be! What is in the believer is not Satan but his own inbred nature, which our Lord came to destroy.

As long as the justified soul is walking in all the Light the Holy Spirit has revealed, this rebellious nature is covered by our Lord's imputed righteousness. This Light will lead to Sanctification that will purify this mutinous nature by imparting holy righteousness.

Imputed righteousness covers the justified person just as it does a child until the child reaches accountability age. At this point the child becomes responsible for what decisions are made. Which is always true with a justified believer who walks in all the Light given. This holds true until the believer is aware of the sinfulness of his inbred sin. When this happens; he is in the valley of decision. He makes the choice, is he going to surrender the old nature for cleansing, or is he going to refuse the Light the Holy Spirit is so faithfully revealing? Putting the decision off will not work. Eventually the Lord will push the battling soul in the corner and say, you must decide now. Time has been given to weigh all the costs.

Who can tell the results of the refusal of holy Light? Spiritual regression is certain. The door is open for all kinds of the sins of the spirit, bitterness, criticism, further rebellion and a faithful fault finder. To reject Light, is to turn the back on the holy life, which is the only life of victory. We never stay in the same spiritual condition. We are either going forward or backwards. To spurn holy Light, is to go backwards.

Try as the believer may, his best efforts only lead to an up and down spiritual life. It almost appears necessary to live in a confessional booth. Too many professing Christians believe this kind of spiritual roller coaster is the only way to live the Christian life. Multitudes falter, others' defeats cause them to give up. To these, there must be an awareness that if God is the God of all creation, He certainly can give victory over the horrors of Spiritual defeat. Yes, it will take your all, but there is where the victory is.

EXCELLENCE

When the soul burns with the fire of the Holy Spirit, there is something in the regenerated man that refuses to settle for anything less than soul excellence. The inward conflict will never satisfy the burning desire to please the living God. God made man bigger and more majestic than the lowly nature that craves for its carnal appetites to be nursed. The soul is made to hunger and thirst for glory's riches, and cannot be quenched with anything less.

Maynard James puts the demand for excellence and purity in these words: "Can a Christian's heart be filled with God the Holy Ghost and still retain indwelling sin? As well might we ask if a room can be completely flooded with light and yet have darkness lurking inside. God is light and love:

where He reigns there can be neither darkness nor hatred. Therefore, the heart that is filled or baptized with the Spirit, must, of necessity, be cleansed from all the darkness and foulness of indwelling sin." (*Facing the Issue*, p. 36)

The yearning for spiritual excellence drives the soul for more and more of our holy God. God's pilgrim cry is in the words of the poet:

"My idols I cast at They feet,
My all I return Thee who gave;
This moment the work is complete,
For Thou art almighty to save.

"O Savior, I dare to believe,
Thy blood for my cleansing I see;
And, asking in faith, I receive
Salvation, full, present, and free."

Bishop Peck would reply to those who say this spiritual excellence (holiness), is possible and worthy, but is it necessary, considering the price? "Many will admit that it is desirable, that it transcends in importance all other objects of interest to an immortal soul. They are convinced that it is possible; for they do not dare to limit the power of God, nor the efficacy of His remedies.

"But they do not regard it as necessary, as indispensable. They incline to resolve the whole into a question of expediency or convenience. And, as it is inconvenient to give thorough attention to it; inconvenient to part with many cherished worldly gratifications; inconvenient to be wholly and only Christians, they waive it, and think they have committed no wrong, violated no law, run no risk!" (*The Central Idea of Christianity*, Bishop Jesse Peck, p. 27)

Many prefer struggling on, dealing with the pain that spiritual defeat brings, and sensing the knowledge their spiritual aspirations are slipping little by little. Soon they become accustomed to living in the lower spiritual realm where standards are subordinate to personal gratification, never tasting the full blessing of victory that gives the motive purity and the heavenly rest for which the redeemed seek and long.

John Wesley reminds the willful rejecters of God's excellence who excuse themselves because they do not live habitually in sin, only occasionally, that he finds no place in God's Word where this type of life style is excusable in these following words: "Habitually! Whence us that? I read it not. It is not written in the Book. God plainly saith, 'He doth not commit sin;' and thou addest habitually! Who art thou that mendest the oracles of God? – that 'addest to the words of this Book?' Beware, I beseech thee, lest God, 'add to thee all the plagues that are written therein!'" (Quote from p. 58 Ibid., sec. 5)

To stop short of excellence, is to rebuff God's best for His children. To harbor enmity against God, is to totally miss the creative purpose of God to enjoy the greatest privilege our God has to offer redeemed mankind. The call to excellence makes man aware that he is especially made to be far above all the other creatures of the universe, solely created for heaven with eternity in mind.

The sainted Commissioner Brengle admonishes us: "This work was begun in you when you were converted. You gave up your sins. You were in some measure separated from the world; the love of God was in some degree shed abroad in your heart, and wholly, you also feel that there are yet roots of bitterness within; quickness of temper, stirrings of pride, too great a sensitiveness to praise or blame, shame of the Cross, love of ease, worldly mindedness, and the like. These must be taken away before your heart can be made clean, and love the God and man made perfect, and the Holy Spirit have all His way in you. When this is done, you will experience what the Bible calls holiness, and which the Salvation Army rightly teaches is the birthright of all God's dear children." (*The Way of Holiness*, p. 7)

The inner demand for excellence makes man say "forgiveness is incomplete; it must be matched by holiness and Christian perfection." Salvation is never entire without a holy life. Can even a nominal Christian deny this? For the very first mark on human character is that God enables those who have so experienced this matchless Grace can avoid committing willful sin.

Excellence has its beginning and must continue its maturity. Once this is the basic part of life it becomes habitual holy living. Excellence is putting every part of our being under God's control and direction. Every thing else is counter productive.

A young man got up in the meeting and said: "Since the Lord converted me I never wanted any bad thing, but there was something in me that did." This truly describes all believers who know not the cleansing power of the Holy Spirit. "A little boy got blessedly saved, and was very happy and good for some time. But one day he came to his mother and said, "Mamma, I'm tired of living this way." The mother asked him about this matter. The little fellow said: "I want to be good all the time. You tell me to go and do things, and I go and do them; but I feel angry inside, and I want to be good all the time." (Ibid p. 16)

To be torn between the drag of the low spiritual life and the pull of the high, is a condemnation that is too weighty for the soul to carry. The believer is feeling the wretchedness of that one that cried out: "O wretched man that I am, who shall deliver me from this body of death." Instead of victory, guilt deepens, and holy judgment settles down to pronounce the verdict already known, for he knows what he is.

There is an intense desire for the rest of perfect love. The powerful internal conviction cries with the Psalmist: "Create in me a clean heart, O God." Multitudes have laid life and soul on the line with this cry from the heart, and found glorious victory over that depraved inner nature.

John Gardner in his book on Excellence says: "Whoever I am or whatever I am doing, some kind of excellence is within my reach." The Spiritual man knows there is no markdown on excellence, and fully realizes God has made available the possibilities to achieve man's deepest desire. God's excellence clearly reveals the inner poverty and empty self effort. There is a traitor within. Remember the Trojan horse they captured, thinking it to be a prize, but the enemy was on the inside. The enemy opened the gates from the inside and the Greeks poured in. Troy was defeated, because they were unaware the enemy was within.

Out of sheer desperation the believer is driven to the Savior for the answer to the inbred sin's problem. He is now willing and ready to gather what he is, and what he hopes to be, bringing that contemptible self to be nailed to the Cross for its crucifixion. Laying all on the altar to be sacrificed for His glory and His glory alone, his faith is ready to move him into the position to receive Sanctifying Grace. Such surrender will allow him to step into the land filled with milk and honey, God's promised land.

CHAPTER VIII

SANCTIFYING FAITH
Why sanctifying faith

On the back of the check the waitress placed on the table were the words: "our goal is excellence." Blazed on the soul of man are these same words. Wesley said: "These convinced me more than ever, of the absolute impossibility of being half a Christian; and I determined, through his grace, (the absolute necessity of which I was deeply sensible of,) to be all devoted to God, to give him all my soul, my body, and substance." (*Works*, XI, p. 367)

Again writing to Charles his passion is revealed: "O insist everything on full redemption, receivable by faith alone! Consequently to be looked for now. . .Press the instantaneous blessing. . .Again he wrote to Freeborn Garretson in 1765 with the same urgency: "The more explicitly and strongly you press all believers to aspire after full sanctification, as attainable now by simple faith, the more the whole work of God will prosper." (Letter to Charles Wesley, 1766)

Man cannot be content to see men as trees or look through dull meaningless spiritual perception and get a correct view of God and heaven. It is the soul's yearning to enter into the splendor of His glories within. This hunger is never satisfied being on the outside looking in. But if there is no desire, no longing for the high and the holy, no interest in pursuing perfect love, no willingness to study the doctrine in the holy scriptures, no aspirations to live a holy life or experience heart cleansing, there is nothing man can do, but pray. It is certain God will not force man against his will. If we are to love with all our being, it can only be done by the will being free to do so.

If the seeker is in the state of carnal refusal toward exposure to Biblical truth, there is convincing certainty there will be no growth, regardless of the effort to control the inner turmoil. There may be those that feel they need to put greater effort into trying to clean out the carnality that is at the root of the problem and ignore the fact that inbred sin is beyond personal effort, suppression, or a life battle the two nature theory presents. This cleansing can only take place by presenting the whole being as a living sacrifice, and the Holy Spirit actually cleansing the old nature, giving holy purity free rein, without any restrictions. Carnality restricts God from complete whole possession.

THE HOLY LIFE IS ATTAINABLE NOW!

In the above statement, hopefully the personal effort was not to be interpreted to mean there would be no effort needed in seeking Sanctification's work of Grace. There is a definite difference between trying to work to defeat carnality, through personal struggle, rather than seeking God to do what is not possible for human effort to do. It has the same interpretation and result that a sinner would have, if he thought good works and great effort would develop into becoming a born again Christian.

In regeneration there must be convincing growth in Grace, but this does not mean an individual grows into Sanctification. There can a growth and concern before becoming a Christian, but there must be a time when each person presents himself to be saved from his sins, and then God acts, and that soul knows God has saved him. The same approach is needed when it comes to dealing with the carnal nature and Sanctification, but this experience is now sought from a forgiven state, as a child of God. Because of being a child of God, the soul is in the right spiritual condition, and has walked in the Light to pursue the Holy Spirit to cleanse the nature from inbred sin.

This is not an experience pursued and never obtained, but it is as immediate as the desire is to have it now. No one will cross their Jordan at the same place as another, but whenever Jordan is crossed to experience the land of milk and honey, faith must part the waters, and readiness to believe that whatever enemy is in the mountains ahead, the God that led through the wilderness, is the God who is greater than any enemy that will be encountered. It does not mean there will no longer be any battles, but it does mean the carnal nature no longer controls the uncontrollable. Now the enemy is on the outside, and his efforts must come from without rather than from within. Before he starts his trouble, he already has two strikes against him. The faith of the believer has reached for the ultimate, and God will not disappoint that.

There will be always those few who continually speak in glowing terms about how wonderful everything is. It would appear, they never have faced temptation, never encountered a battle with the satanic forces, never experienced a crushing blow, never had a problem in the family, and on we could go. I don't know where they have been, for that is not real life. Life is filled with heartaches and over whelming circumstances. Just because an individual is sold out for God does not mean there will never be trials. All the Apostles but one was put to death by those who were advocates of brutal hatred, and if they think they can take a definite stand for Biblical righteousness and not drink these bitter dregs, they must be living on a deserted island.

But the reality is, in the midst of every rough rugged situation, God's child is never alone in that painful conflict. The Lord does not wander off when the battle gets ugly. This is a partnership that only man can break, and that will be through willful disobedience. Past victories reassure His continual faithfulness. Obedience is always rewarded with the consciousness of God's presence and blessing.

MAN APPROPRIATING WHAT GOD HAS AVAILABLE!

God and man compliment one another, as man learns to appropriate what God has available. Man can have the most fertile ground there is, but if he just stands and looks and admires it, he'll never have the potatoes needed to feed the family, or the wheat to make his bread. God has placed in that ground the necessary ingredients, gives the sunshine and the rain, but man must appropriate what God has already given and plant the seeds. In that seed He has placed life, but it must be surrounded with the proper components already given. This is the partnership necessary to sustain life.

In the same way, God has unmeasurable power that will produce the satisfaction the soul craves. But man must apply God's Grace to his need. There will never be any fruit until he does. His cleansing power is available, but spiritual life depends on what is done with it by each individual. It is imperative that the soul goes after it, with all desire and will. Appropriate what God has already given, and abundant life is yours.

At this point, the impelling urge for the Holy Life has now broken down the self-will, to will to die to self and live for God only. But this inducing desire and conviction does not rise out of a heart that is rebellious and living in willful disobedience. But rather it spills from a heart that yearns to do only God's will. He longs to be purged from the unbearable pain that comes when the carnal nature overruns the inner being, and causes untold self-condemnation. The seeking soul has arrived at the crisis where no sacrifice will be too great, no cost too excessive to find the peace and victory the spiritual being demands. The battleground is surrendered.

The mandate for purity of heart has all the elements of desire, will, purpose, and surrender wrapped up in the Sanctifying faith that appeals with wholeness of heart for the clean and pure heart. The intensity deepens until there is a definite encounter with the Holy Spirit doing the purging of the carnal nature. Brother Hames says: "There is no command for gradual honesty. Let him that stole steal no more. An instantaneous honesty." If there is any intention of doing business with God, it is a call to lay down all arms, with a willingness to sign an unconditional surrender, NOW!

J. A. Wood says the soul seeking Sanctification now asks these searching questions.

"Do I believe that God is able to sanctify me?
Do I believe that He is willing to sanctify me?
Do I believe that He promised to sanctify me?
Do I believe that having promised, He is able and willing to do it now, on conditions of my faith?
Do I then, seeing all this, believe that He now will do it – now, this moment?
Am I now committing all, and trusting in Christ?
If you are, it is done. O that God may aid your trembling faith and give you purity this moment!" (*Perfect Love*, p. 62)

This is the conviction of the searching longing heart. There is a determination that nothing – no, not hell itself, with all its demons – shall stop your quest. The act of complete consecration is an utter separation from the carnal to the sacred. It is the ultimate of the rich young ruler selling all he had. His possessions must not, could not stand between him and His God. It is everything, or nothing, as far as God is concerned. Any soul that tries to give Him less will be totally disappointed.

Jonathan Edwards said it this way: "I have this day solemnly renewed my covenant and dedication. I have been before God, and given myself and all that I am and have to Him, so that I am not in any respect my own, and can claim no right to myself – to this understanding, to this will, these affections; and have no right to this body – to this tongue, these hands, these feet; no right to these senses. I have given every power to God, so that for the future I will claim no right to myself."

Such a seeking heart, must be ready for the Lord to nail him to his personal cross. There is a willingness to openly embrace any shame that is to be heaped upon him for enfolding God's Holy Standards. The old hymn tells it this way: "His reproach I'll gladly bear." Ugly humiliation is easily encountered when undiluted Biblical standards become absolutes; labels can castigate character when unadulterated God given convictions become a normal way of life; condemning discredit will be used by spreading the charge of extremism, ultra right. and accusations that this stand is nothing more than depicting yourself as a self-righteousness prude. How many have, and will, back away from this type of thorny cross. But if the believer wishes to go anywhere with the Lord God being master, he must be ready and willing to bear the shame that is certain to come. Are you ready for that? If not, don't step forward. Too many are in His service that have not paid this price, and have become sounding brass and tinkling cymbals.

Bishop Foster asks the seeker to check with his will to see if his will is willing to agree with doing only His Master's will. Does his will want to submit to self-denial, entire devotion to the Living God, or does his will have another agenda that does not include such demanding sacrifice? Is this will ready to forfeit self interest, self ambitions, its own self will, your family, your reputation, every thing materially possessed for the sole purpose of doing God's will?

The Gospel admonishes those who seek Sanctification to be ready to walk the unknown road. It will take all, but all is too small of a word. This yielding mandates the unlimited whole. Don't expect Spiritual victory if less is offered. This is an individual matter. Many will try to explore a different road to escape the anguish of the adversity found on this road, hoping against hope that there is another way that has a lighter load, with less struggles.

Sanctifying Faith stands, viewing the battlefield, seeing the wounds of those who faltered, hearing the cries of those who hesitated and are now too weary to fight the good fight of faith. Struggling against faithlessness, discord and confusion; they must consider, are they willing to pay the price for Spiritual victory after pondering the horrors of the fallen who sought an easier road that didn't demand so much? No one can make that decision for you. There must be a separation from all that is carnal, including what God given talents you may have, or intellectual powers acquired and a willingness to devote them to execute His holy will, only. Don't start the building, if you first haven't considered the cost to finish it.

Sanctifying Faith has its base in these words written by Dr. Steele and confirmed by J. A. Wood: "Make an entire Consecration of yourself to God. . .Searching and surrender, and research and surrender again, until you get every vestige of self upon the altar of consecration. There is no sanctification without entire sanctification." (*Perfect Love*, p. 61 Dr. Steele and J. A. Wood)

Sanctifying Faith must have an adequate foundation from which to operate. This would be impossible without entire surrender of everything known and unknown. Therefore, it is necessary to run up and down the whole being so not one jot or tittle is left unsurrendered. The event of Spiritual dying is at hand, with crucifixion of self the next step. Thorough preparation must be taken. My mother had things labeled, tied together, and separated. She was preparing to die. What about it? Is there a readiness, a separation of the mind with all its faculties, the soul with all its potential, for time and eternity, the will with its power to choose life or death, the appetites with their various tastes, relationships that have the possibility of being your downfall, are they primed to die to and for all future personal goals to enhance any private achievement that does not promote His glory?

The scripture is very definite, that God's call is for now. "Be ye Holy" means nothing at all if it doesn't mean now. It is clearly present tense, not at the point of physical death. If I am commanded to love my neighbor, be truthful, and honest, it can not mean anything else, but at this present time. Again, we are commanded to "put off. . .the old man, which is corrupt. . . and put on the new man, which after God is created in righteousness and true holiness." (Eph. 4:22-24) We are directed to be "filled with the Spirit," and not to have any part in "anger, wrath, malice, blasphemy, filthy communication out of your mouth." With every command, God must give the power to have victory now to fulfill that command. There is no power if the will does not will to receive it.

FAITH BECOMES ANCHORED IN GOD'S POWER TO MEET THE SOUL'S NEED!

There can be all the necessary searching out in every area, but if faith is not activated, the soul will never rise above the surrender itself. Faith would be useless if the abandonment of self was not done first, but when all is placed on the altar, faith must set in. In Wesley's *Brief Thoughts on Christian Perfection*, he states: "as to the manner, I believe this perfection is always wrought in the soul by a single act of faith: consequently, in an instant." (p. 136)

In *Wesley and Sanctification* by Harold Lindstrom he writes: ". . .the faith by which a man partakes of complete sanctification implies conviction of God's promise and power to redeem him from all sin and perfect him in love and of His power and willingness to do this without delay, to do it now. To this is added the conviction that God actually does do it." (p. 117)

Sanctifying Faith is now willing to match man's diabolical depravity against the cleansing stream that flowed at Calvary to give victory over this defeating nature. This faith now is demanding complete triumph over the fallen nature and the Light to penetrate the darkness that has thrown over the soul. Soul liberation is the heart cry.

THE NEED FOR SANCTIFICATION!

John Wesley said: "We do not know of a single instance, in any place, of a person receiving at one and the same moment, remission of sins, the abiding witness of the Spirit, and a new and clean heart."

Adam Clarke remarks: "I have been twenty three years a traveling preacher and have been acquainted with some thousands of Christians during that time, who were in different states of grace; and I never, to my knowledge met with a single instance, where God both justified and sanctified at the same time."

Witnessing to the Spirit and Sanctification Polycarp, the martyr, the Bishop of Smyrna said: "He who is possessed of love is free from all sin."

John Chrysostom, the golden-tongued preacher declared that "to obtain such power and to receive forgiveness of sins are not one and the same."

WITNESSING TO SANCTIFICATION

Matthew Henry, the noted commentator, says regarding the prayer of Jesus in John 17: "Jesus prayed for all that are his that they might be sanctified. He could not for every claim, own them as His, either employ them in His service or present them to His Father if they be not sanctified."

Richard Watson, a renowned theologian said: "We have already spoken of regeneration, adoption, and the witness of the Spirit; we proceed to another experience as distinctly marked and as graciously promised in the scriptures; namely, the entire sanctification or perfection of believers."

Charles Wesley sang:

"Speak the second time, 'Be Clean!'
Take away my inbred sin;
Every stumbling-block remove,
Cast it out by perfect love."

D. L. Moody relates that two ladies informed him that they were praying that he, "might receive the power of the Spirit." Moody said he thought he had all that was needed, but soon there came a hunger into his soul. One day on a street in New York City, God filled him with His spirit. Of that Moody says: "Oh, what a day! I cannot describe it; I seldom refer to it; it is almost too sacred an experience to name." Then he said: "I went to preaching again. The sermons were not different; I did not present any new truths; and yet hundreds were converted. I would not now be placed back where I was before the blessed experience if you give me all the world."

Now Sanctifying Faith says – "The personal spiritual experience demands it, God commands it, and others verify its truth by actual experience, thus, God is no respecter of person, the holy heart is for me, now." Sanctifying Faith is the step needed to God's act of Sanctification, cleansing the depraved nature that so long plagued the soul.

CHAPTER IX

SANCTIFICATION

What is sanctification and why is it necessary?

The demand that man's inner being compels is for excellence, that refuses to stop at the spiritual step of regeneration. Spiritual excellence is not possible as long as carnality is discharging its enmity against God. No one knows this better than the one that is doing it. He becomes acutely aware the Regenerated life is not the Holiness about which the Bible speaks. The Holy God can not condone the resentments that surface all too frequently, nor the exploding temper that shames the testimony, nor the bitterness that is eating away at the spiritual vine. In proportion to the depth of this painful conviction, in that proportion sanctifying faith will be applied to the pure heart. This conviction can reach such depth that there can be a loss of appetite, or the night can be spent in sleepless restlessness.

At a time like this, the loudspeakers in the soul can be blasting these words: "follow peace with all men, and holiness, without which no man shall see the Lord." (Heb.12;1-4) There is an absorbing entrancement in the regenerated man's soul to measure up to the standards to which God has called him. But there is nothing more defeating than to know the ego is dominating the decisive situations, allowing the crippled soul to continually fall short.

All too many times the spiritually awakened regenerated man does not see the repulsive and hedonistic reality his sensual nature is, until he sees its ugliness as God sees it. Seeing himself, he loathes what he is. No excuse or alibi will remove the heart's despair. But the Holy Spirit can cleanse all the chaos and dilemma that is manufactured by human depravity. Thank God, He does not desire that the soul remains in this state, drinking dregs, while the stream is gushing forth Living Water.

Reinhold Niebur discusses – "the labyrinthian depths of the conscious," which is saying, the passage through life is an intricate structure of interconnecting passages through which it is difficult to find one's way. This is one of the basic reasons man needs God. Natural man is lost in his darkness, aimlessly groping to find his way through life's maze. If the Holy Spirit is not directing and controlling the destiny, man then likens himself to being in a dark cave with no guide, and many passages going all directions, not knowing which one will lead to light and life.

The Bible has declared God's way from the beginning. Theologians and the mainstream denominations would not be so far afield if they would have adhered to the historic scriptural position. The Bible has a very pessimistic view on man's nature apart from Calvary's cleansing agency.

God's man is never satisfied with merely being a seeker. He must be a possessor. In more cases than not, the enemy uses terms to build prejudices that are meant to confuse the seeker. It is difficult to sift through all the bewilderment and mayhem to focus on the holy goal sought. But don't allow terms to side track from the everlasting purpose that is burning within.

There are any number of names given to sanctification, both Biblical and non-biblical, but the meaning is essentially the same. By listing some, possibly it will help the mind and heart to come to a singleness of purpose: Holiness – purity – Christian perfection – perfect love – fullness of Christ – the baptism of the Holy Spirit – the full assurance of faith – complete surrender – wholeness – entire sanctification – second blessing – the deeper life, etc.

Whatever name or term is used, the meaning is Christian Perfection, which has its definition wrapped up in the first and second commandments. John Wesley encountered this sinister move to twist these terms beyond or below the Christian concept, so he records in his journal Tuesday, June 27,1770, these words, from a letter, "to a pious and sensible woman: "By Christian perfection I mean, (1) Loving God with all our heart. Do you object to this? I mean (2) a heart and life all devoted to God. Do you desire less? I mean (3) regaining the whole image of God. What objection to this? I mean (4) having all the mind that was in Christ. Is this going too far? I mean (5) walking uniformly as Christ walked. And this surely no Christian will object to. If anyone means anything more or anything else by perfection, I have no concern with it. But if this is wrong, yet what need of this heat about it, this violence, I had almost said, fury of opposition, carried so far as even to lay out anything with this man, or that woman, who professes it?" (*The Journal of John Wesley*, Moody Press, 1951, p. 305)

Certainly, Biblical language seems to be less misleading, and more authoritative. If Biblical terms are still offensive, then this must be taken up with the Lord Himself. There is no miracle in the terms, it is the act of the Holy Spirit that does the cleansing. Numbers of people can mouth the correct phraseology and associate with like-minded people but know nothing of the actual cleansing act itself.

The number of times a term is used would tell us about how important the scriptural inspiration consider it to be, and how compelling the doctrine is. Compare the significance placed on "Justification" and "Perfection." Justify and its derivatives are used 74 times, and pardon and its derivatives 17 times. While perfect or perfection is used 50 times in relation to human character: and Holy and its derivatives 120 times. However it is weighed, honorable men will not deny our God has called all peoples to live pure and holy lives. The unsullied soul's thirst can't be quenched with anything less than heart Holiness. Our God made us that way, and no satanic effort can change that. The human being is too big for the slush and mire that drops him below the God image he is to exalt.

A MIXED HOLINESS IS MORE PREFERABLE THAN THE BIBLICAL KIND!

The average Christian wants to be holy, but the price of self-denial is too high. There is attachment to the good life, the bank account, the pension plan, "the security" that these things appear to bring. Thus, there is little need for trusting God for any need when all this is already on the platter. What can the Lord offer more, but a detestable Cross from which most professing Christians are fleeing. Present day belief is brought down to personal opinion. Biblical authoritativeness is no longer dominating personal decisions, but still there is an effort on most to be some kind of a Christian. The name Christian still holds a certain kind of respectability. What honorable person would want to be considered a heathen, which some regard being opposite to Christian.

The reality of the living conditions under the bondage of mixed holiness, (but there is no such thing, although there are those who have invented it to their own deception), holds the threat of total spiritual destruction. Mr. Wesley describes such a predicament preceding the Sanctifying cleansing in these words: "Until this universal change was wrought in his soul, all his holiness was mixed, he was humble, but not entirely; his humility was mixed with pride; he was meek, but his meekness was frequently interrupted by anger, or some uneasy and turbulent passion. His love of God was frequently dampered by the love of his neighbor, by evil surmising, or some thought, is not temper, contrary to love. His will was not wholly melted down into the will of God; but although in general he could say, 'I come not to do my own will, but the will of him that sent me;' yet now and then nature rebelled, and could not clearly say, 'Lord, not as I will, but as thou wilt.'" (*Wesley's Works*, Vol. II, p. 222)

God did not make us for a mixture, but for singleness of purpose, any thing less puts the soul and God at cross intent. This can only bring spiritual chaos. The God image drives the honest seeker to search for Divine deliverance. The inner conflict bears heavily upon a piercing conscience. Only the cleansing act of the Holy Spirit can lift this weight.

YOU CANNOT RECEIVE WHAT YOU DON'T BELIEVE TO BE POSSIBLE!

For any one to receive the Sanctifier, he or she must believe he can be Sanctified. "He that cometh to God must believe that He is, and that He is a rewarder of them that diligently seek Him." (Heb. 11:6) This faith is surrendered to the Master to meet the soul's need as God sees it. The will, the mind, the appetites, the ambitions, all are yielded entirely. There is full assurance that being mastered by our Lord is all the soul wants and needs.

This step of faith and obedience recognizes God can do the cleansing work to bring purity, and settle the sin problem in the unholy nature. This type of compliance puts the soul in the proper position to allow God to act.

Care must be taken that feeling is not what is being sought. Emotions may be a part of the experience but is not the primary part, and should not replace definite faith that brings the act into being, which allows God to do things His way. There is nothing more important than to want most to glorify Him in whatever way He chooses. The seeker no longer dictates policy that has been turned over to the Master without reservations. "Positional Sanctification is the spiritual state of the believer, being in the Sanctified state at the present time. "Paul...unto the church of God which is at Corinth, to them that are sanctified (now) in Christ Jesus, called saints, with all that call upon the name of our Lord Jesus Christ in every place, their Lord and ours." (1 Cor. 1:1-3) This is not a position we walk into, or grow into, it is God's definite act that moves into that position.

IT IS POSSIBLE TO RESIST POSITIONAL SANCTIFICATION !

It is not only possible, multitudes of professing Christians do. There are always less than favorable consequences that accompany such resistance. There are various stages of denying and open opposition. No two will face the factual need the same way. One may procrastinate, hoping conviction and desire will be buried by time. Another can allow cold indifference to smother any up reach for the high and the holy. While another can rationalize this precious Light until the Light blinds so that this spiritual truth is never known. Of course, there is always open rebellion when conviction is so cutting, the ugly nature will lash out into carnal decisions and actions, sinking to a low level of wickedness that they never ever thought would be said or done. Their very outrage reveals the need for that which is being fought against.

Whatever the category in which each is found, it is sure that the real spiritual state cannot be covered very long. Always the true self will emerge. It is just as the seed when sown. It all depends on the type of soil on which the seed falls. Its fruit bearing relies upon what is there to nourish the seed. If the ground resists the seed, it will destroy the seed's worth. Little does the carnal soul realize the seriousness of rejecting this Light.

In Wesley's day he met open resistance in almost every segment of society. A clergyman preached against the stand the Methodists were taking by painting them as black as devils, closing his sermon with these words: "I have no time to finish now! Next Sunday I will give you the rest." But by the next Sunday he was so stricken that he never preached again.

Challenging Biblical holiness, always has its repercussions. They may not be as evident in this life as it was with the priest who led a mob in attacking the Methodists in Wesley's day. The next Sunday he fell dead at the altar of his church. There are different depths of resistance, but all have the same end results. "He that rejecteth, rejecteth not man, but God who giveth his Holy Spirit unto you." (A. V. I Thess. 4:8)

IS SANCTIFICATION SCRIPTURAL?

Is that to which God calls us anything but Scriptural? "For God hath not called us unto uncleanness, but unto holiness." (1 Thess. 4:7) God never calls us to the unholy or the unrighteous, but His call is always to purity and Holiness. Bishop Foster lists a few of the scriptures that teach positional sanctification or its experience. Ps. 37:37; Job 8:20; Mark 6:20; Rom. 6:22; Rom. 8:2-4; Luke 1:6; Gal. 2:20; 1 John 4:17; Rev. 14:5; Isa. 6:5-7; 2 Cor.7:1; Heb. 6:1 & 12:14; Matt. 5:48; John 17:17; Rom. 15:16; Eph. 5:26; 2 Tim. 2:21; Heb. 13:12; I Peter 1:2; Lev. 11:45; Luke 1:74; 1 Peter 1:16; 2 Peter 3:11; and many more. There are also the negative verification such as "without offense," "without rebuke," "without blame," "Free from sin." The whole Book calls for man to be holy. Without the stream flowing through the whole scripture, there is no foundation for a doctrine. Philosophers and theologians can self create anything the human mind can concoct, but if these liberal visionaries have no scriptural backing, they are empty and without spiritual foundation. Of course, it must be understood they would say the Bible has no more validity than any other book, completely undercutting the authentic authority of the scriptures.

Dr. Henry Sheldon, a Methodist Theologian writes: "A rational warrant for denying the possibility of entire sanctification in this life being thus wanting, the ground of denial must be found, if discovered at all, in revelation. It must be proved that the scriptures teach that it is outside of the divine ability or the divine purpose to consummate the sanctification of any subject of grace before the article of death. Calvinists are hindered, of course, by their postulate from assuming that it is beyond the divine ability to do this, and non-Calvinists must needs despair of sustaining this assumption from the scriptures, in the face of such words as those of Paul, which describe God as 'able to do exceeding abundantly above all that we ask or think.' It remains then to deduce from the Scriptures that it is outside the divine purpose or not part of the divine economy to bring any one to the point of entire sanctification in this life. But who has ever made a deduction of this sort which has even the appearance of legitimacy.

Various passages show indeed, that every man has unmistakable occasion to include himself in the ranks of sinners when his life is taken as a whole. Not one of these, however, gives the faintest indication that its author meant to teach that in no case can sin be entirely put away before the separation of the soul and body. Take for example, this declaration of John: "If we say we have no sin, we deceive ourselves, and the truth is not in us." What an eccentricity of exegesis to suppose that this teaching is a necessary continuance in sin, when the next verse reads: "If we confess our sins, He is faithful and just to forgive us our sins, and to cleanse us from all unrighteousness." (Henry Sheldon, *System of Christian Doctrine*, p. 465)

OBJECTIONS TO SANCTIFICATION!

Any experience so personalized and possessing with so great a cost to the human ego, can not be perpetuated without objections. The more intense the demands upon the self life, the more violent the objections. Naturally all of them cannot be listed, but rather than trying to avoid them, we hope to list the ones that appear to be used most frequently.

It is impossible for a holy life to be lived or obtained in this life. How many times have you encountered that one? In spite of what the scripture says, "Be ye holy, for I am holy," there are those who have settled into the carnal life, and are convinced this is the normal Christian life. But how could our just and holy God command us to be that which He knows is impossible to achieve. If this command can not be achieved then the attributes and the very character of God will have to be reversed. All that we know Him to be, such injustice would not allow Him to be. There is no way an honest growing believer can ignore such a present tense direct command, "Be ye holy, for I am holy," nor "God hath not called us to uncleanness, but unto holiness."

There is another objection that says holiness is no more than a cloak of self-righteousness. If that is so, then God is guilty of creating a sect of self-righteous prudes, that want to be placed on some pedestal with the multitudes groveling at their feet. But the holiness our God promotes is, God first, others second, and whatever comes next falls in line. This life takes on the role of "love slave." The menial task is not considered to be subservient, but done to God's glory.

Those also object who claim that there is a prejudice associated with the high standards. What are the standards for which the objector advocates? Anything lower than Biblical standards will disgrace Calvary and its cost. Multitudes have decided they could take it upon themselves to replace the Biblical standard with their own, only to find "it is hard to kick against pricks." Their road has led them to view the hopelessness of the blind leading the blind. The ditch is filled. Those who have made the choice before them, are caught wallowing in their shame as death approaches. There is nothing more pitiful than to be forced to look back over life with emptiness that bitter regret can never fill. For it does matter what we do with Christ.

Only the Lord knows the vast numbers who have withered under the cross, for any number of reasons, but the contempt shown by their peers who have done the same thing is unendurable. Its pain is only known by those who have made their own rules.

Cowardly men cringe at the thought of taking a stand for the holy life, or even associating with any thing that resembles Holiness, to which our God states: "without Holiness we can not see God." We are admonished by brother Wesley to be men of courage and honor, regardless of what our cross may involve, or how rugged the way. "By silence one who has attained to perfect love, might avoid many crosses, which will naturally and necessarily issue the soul. If, therefore, such a one were to confer with flesh and blood, he would be entirely silent. But this could not be done with a clear conscience; for undoubtedly he ought to speak. Men do not light a candle to put it under a bushel; much less does the all-wise God. He does not raise up a monument of His power and love, to hide it from all mankind: rather He intends it to be a general blessing to those who are simple of heart. He designs thereby not barely the happiness of that individual person, but the animating and encouraging others to follow after the same blessing. His will is 'that many shall see it' and rejoice, 'and put their trust in the Lord.'" (*Wesley's Works*, Vol. XI, p. 382)

Many modern day Samsons have betrayed the source of their power, and now this has become the normal way to live their powerless lives, not even aware the Lord has departed. So often, the deterioration has been so gradual they still assume the power is there.

How strong the temptation grows when the Holiness person is by-passed by others who avoided any particular Holiness stand. Satan makes sure to point out the one who stepped ahead, or received a D.D. because of being appointed to some position. Achievement is seldom based on spirituality, usually on status. To most, the temptation or cost is too great, the humiliation is too degrading to pay that type of price. It is easier to assign the doctrine of Sanctification to the back burner, or exclude the doctrine all together. There are those who are so timid they apologize for it being scriptural. By opposing this basic doctrine, the authority of the scripture is undercut. The gospel can not be saved without its message.

The objections would not be complete without adding three given by the noted Dr. Sangster's complaint: "(1) It involves the use of words with a limited meaning, the limitations of which may not be clear to the people who hear the witness. (2) Such a claim is hard to harmonize with a moment of life. (3) It involves the awful danger of presumption and pride and self-induced spiritual blindness." (*The Path To Perfection*, pp. 164-167)

Wherever there is the false, there first must be the truth. Is any one or more of these objections going to deter the determined seeking soul who wants deliverance at all cost? Once delivered, the soul refuses to be silent. Can freedom be retained by muzzling its right to speak, or integrity be secured by prejudicing others from seeking a holy heart?

Just because there are those objectors, does that mean that the leper should never speak of his healing, lest there be the possibility the leprosy could break out in some other area of his body. Should we not speak of our marvelous deliverance from sin's mastery of the inner life? Silence declares a denial.

IS THERE A NEED FOR SANCTIFICATION?

Who would dare to even suggest there isn't a vital need for heart purity? Does the regenerated soul encounter the war that arouses enmity against his God, and not be aware there is something radically wrong with the spiritual condition of the heart? Does not inner inspection verify to the honest soul there is no way divided loyalty can please God.

Personal experience corroborates and establishes the justified soul's need for the cleansing that is not possessed. O, so many professing Christians acknowledge their need carnality creates, but do not believe this necessitates a definite act of God to Sanctify, purifying the heart. Forgiveness is for the acts of sins committed, which every justified soul has experienced. If this is the extent of salvation's plan, then why does not this soul have complete victory over the carnal nature? Why, then the temper explosions, the self-centered me first, the anger, the animosity, the resentments that keep building or the bitter unforgiveness that is buried so deep it can't be touched.

Dr. Bert H. Hall points out, "Paul's most common word for Christians is "saints", holy ones, for the Greek term hagios. Both Rudolph Otto and Norman Smith suggest that hagios is the Greek equivalent of the Hebrew godesh, a term that teaches the holiness of God and the holiness of man in the Old Testament. Upon this root term, Paul builds his concepts of sanctification. . .his ideas are deeply rooted in the Old Testament revelation of God, a revelation that tells us what God is like and what man can become. . .

Dr. Hall notes, in I Thessalonians Paul uses three different words to teach the meaning of sanctification. In 3:13 he exhorts, "and the Lord make you to increase and abound in love one toward another. . .to the end that he may establish your hearts unblamable in holiness (hagisoune) before our God and Father." In 4:3 he uses the term hagiosmos, "for this is the will of God even your sanctification" and repeats the term twice more in the context. In 5:23 he uses the verb hagiasai, "and the very God of peace sanctify you wholly." Each of these terms are related by derivation to the basic adjective hogios, meaning "holy," "undefiled," "pure." Each is rooted in the Old Testament concept of holiness which speaks of the nature of God and the gift to man. But basically it is the context that suggests differences in the meaning of these terms. Three different facets of the one gem appear." (*The Pauline Doctrine of Sanctification*, Bert Hall)

God's call is never to uncleanness but always to Holiness. The whole mainstream in God's Word vindicates this truth. Anything less limits Calvary. Who would dare to venture giving any limitations on our God's atoning sacrifice? Then this Doctrinal subject needs thorough scriptural investigation. This quotation from Bishop Foster invokes the demand the scripture places on man's opportunity to be made holy. "The doctrine we contend for is not limited to a bare and questionable place, a doubtful and uncertain existence in the records, but is repletely and abundantly, as well as explicitly, embodied as a cardinal feature throughout the whole system. It breathes in the prophecy, thunders in the law, murmurs in the narrative, whispers in the promises, supplicates in the prayers, resounds in the songs, sparkles in the poetry, shines in the types, glows in the imagery, and burns in the spirit, of the whole scheme, from its alpha to its omega – its beginning to its end. Holiness! Holiness needed! Holiness required! Holiness offered! Holiness attainable! Holiness a present enjoyment, is the progress and completeness of its wondrous theme! It is the truth glowing all over and voicing all through revelation; singing and shouting in all its history, and biography, and poetry, and prophecy, and precept, and promise, and prayer; the great central truth of the system. The truth to elucidate which the system exists. If God has spoken at all it is to aid men to be holy. The wonder is, that all do not see, that any rise up to question, a truth so conspicuous, so glorious, so full of comfort." (*Christian Purity*, Bishop R. S. Foster, p. 9)

This need for Sanctification's purity reaches to the whole of man. His disposition, his spirit, his nature, his mind, his ambitions, his motives and his body which is the temple of the Holy Spirit, mandates this cleansing to bring the soul to the position for holy living. Nothing else is acceptable to God or man. We want to be clean. We are constantly sterilizing, washing, scrubbing, laundering, scouring. Why, we demand cleanliness. So it is with the soul. Everything within man pleads for purity. Does not carnality cause man to despise what he is in his uncleanness?

HOW SOON AFTER JUSTIFICATION MAY THE SEEKER BE SANCTIFIED?

Time is not so much the factor, as being aware of the need. The need is impressed by the Spiritual light that has been received and by the demands of the conscience. Many people have been under conviction for their carnality, but not cognizant of what the solution is. While others will have light on Sanctification before they were converted,.

All were admonished by Mr. Wesley to look for it (sanctification) every moment. There is no way that God's act of cleansing can be received without the consciousness of the need which brings cutting conviction. Wesley is saying man becomes the seeker only when he is under conviction resulting from an inner burning need. This persuasion must engulf the whole being where nothing but God's will matters and no price is too great to pay to be cleansed from this nature that is strangling what spiritual life there is. Wesley again urges all to seek, pray, and hunger for heart purity immediately after the new birth. He warns that to allow the spiritual furor to subside, it will be difficult to bring the passion back to the point where the will, will be ready to want God's will.

Without doubt some have lingered so long outside of Canaan they have lost their desire for the Promised Land. They have gotten used to living beneath the privileges that our God has provided. They have lived in carnal squalor so long, it is considered the normal Christian life. Anything other than this low life, especially holy living, is contrived to be fanaticism. To by-pass the best, is to put the soul at risk by resisting scriptural light. People want the best in a car, tool, or appliance, but will settle for the sordid, emaciated spiritual life. The scripture is very plain: "Thou shalt love the Lord thy God with all thy heart," which is in present tense, which is now. This is so clear that anyone living below this expectation of God's command is of all people most wretched, and condemned for their spiritual poverty.

HOW DO WE RECEIVE SANCTIFICATION?

Sanctification is not gained by the length of time involved in the continual moral struggle, nor is it the persistent contest to subdue moral passions or a carnal spirit, but this blessed experience is the gift of God. A gift freely given only needs to be taken when all conditions are met. Faith believes and takes the gift, and whatever denial or cross He may choose in which His purpose can be fully consonanted. Faith is the core by which we are sanctified being perfected in His love. This love must take up the whole heart, hence no room for sin, the enemy.

Through faith He will bring a clean heart out of an unclean, restoring God's marred image, making pure the motivator that drives the decision making. Faith turns personal will over to God's will, establishing an anchored confidence in God's promised truth. This experience is the divine evidence that faith works in the deepest and most critical area of life. We say with John the Apostle who kept repeating, "I know, I know." It is that knowing that rests the soul. Holy love is seated on the throne, duty no longer drives. Perfect love gives a willingness to please God at the expense of personal preference.

WHEN DOES SANCTIFICATION BEGIN?

It is not that sanctification is some foreign counterpart that has been deceptively thrust into our church doctrine by scheming men, but sanctification is an integrated part of salvation whole. To avoid one step of God's plan is comparable to trying to complete a chain by leaving out one link.

As we have seen, there are steps leading to the door of full salvation, and once we walk through the door, Christ Jesus, at that moment the heart is justified by God's act. These steps must be taken in sequence. After the first step, all other steps move up to Justification, becoming a new creature in Christ. At this point Sanctification starts, proceeding in each step, climax in Sanctification's step, when the Holy Spirit acts and cleanses the heart from its depraved nature.

IS SANCTIFICATION INSTANTANEOUS?

The aorist tense of the verb 'sanctify' denotes singleness of action. This then should be helpful when it comes to understanding the action involved in God's single act of the experience of sanctification. Faith gives access, and God's act is completed. It is evident that no one can purify their own heart, by removing their own inbred sin. Only God can deal with the sin's root. Does our God need to struggle over how or when, or muster up some mystical power before He can act? God being God, is He not adequate for any and every need? Would He leave His child at the mercy of sinful depravity?

Often sanctification is portrayed as a gradual growth that eventually there may be an arrival, but when and where is not known. In fact, what these advocates are saying, sanctification is a growth without any arrival, leaving sanctification a mere growth, with no definite act by God. They seek to make sanctification and maturity synonymous. Real maturity comes after an instantaneous sanctifying act by the Holy Spirit. There needs to be a precise time when the old nature is surrendered, and there is a death to the self life and its ambitions. At this time, the act of sanctification is performed by the cleansing of the carnal nature.

Wesley writing to Garretson 1789: "And it will be well as soon as any of them will find peace with God to exhort them to 'go on the perfection.' The more explicitly and strongly you press all believers to aspire after full sanctification, as attainable now, by faith, the more the whole work of God will prosper."

Wesley writing to two men, Bell and Owen, who denied instantaneous sanctification said: "You have over and over denied instantaneous sanctification to me, but I have known and taught it above these twenty years."

Wesley had doubting Thomases in his day as well. In the course of direct questions to 652 members of the society he discovered that in no case was sanctification wrought gradually, but that in every case it came as an instantaneous work of grace in response to faith in Christ, not only as Savior, but also as sanctifier. He went on to say: "Had the half of these, or one-third, or one and twenty, declared it was gradually wrought in them, I should have believed this, in regard to them, and thought that some were gradually sanctified and some instantaneously, but as I have not found, in so long a space of time, a single person speaking thus; as all who believe they are sanctified, declare with one voice, that the change was wrought in a moment. I cannot but believe, that sanctification is commonly, if not always, an instantaneous work. (Vol. II *Wesley Works*, p. 223)

Multiplied multitudes notarized signatures could be added to these testimonials as receiving sanctification as an instantaneous work of grace.

UNDERSTANDING CHRISTIAN PERFECTION OR SANCTIFICATION!

In John Wesley's letter to Thomas Rankin, he expresses his concern for every one of God's justified children: "I have been rightly thinking a good deal on one point wherein perhaps we have all been wanting. We have not made it a rule as soon as every person is justified to remind them of going on into perfection. This is the very time preferably to all others. They have then the simplicity of little children; they are fervent in spirit, ready to cut off a right hand or pluck out the right eye, but if we once suffer this fervor to subside, we shall find it hard enough to bring them ever again to this point."

The Apostle Paul calls us to Christian perfection in these words: "let us therefore, as many as be perfect be thus minded; and if in any ye be otherwise minded, God shall reveal even this unto you." (Phil. 3:15)

The word for "perfect," (Teleios) is a real stumbling block to many people. There is no reason for controversy since it is used in the scriptures more than the words that don't seem to be so offensive, such as justification, regeneration, conversion or being born again. Prejudice closes the door both spiritually and mentally. The results of preconceived ideas spell certain disaster.

How frequently the scriptures use a term reflects on its importance. The word "perfect" is used more than any other single term to set forth Christian experience. Intelligence then demands that we explore its scriptural meaning and understand its usage in relation to God's demands upon our lives.

"Perfect" in the scripture signifies, "brought to its end, finished, wanting nothing necessary to completeness; perfect. There is no such word as more perfect. Perfect is always complete in itself.

Teleios and its derivatives occur 138 times in the scriptures. More than 50 times it refers to human character under the operation of Grace; 45 times the Israelites were commanded to bring sacrifice "without blemish." Dare the human, bringing himself and present himself for sacrificial service be less perfect than an animal being presented.

The Apostle Paul repeats the command but makes it applicable to redeemed individuals: "I beseech you therefore brethren, by the mercies of God that ye present your bodies a living sacrifice, holy, acceptable unto God, which is your reasonable service." Is there anything more reasonable that our Lord can ask of us?

Our Lord uses Teleios to emphasize man's relationship with Himself – "Be ye therefore perfect even as your Father which is in heaven is perfect." (Matt. 5:48). Again in the account of the rich young ruler – "if thou wilt be perfect go sell that thou hast, and give to the poor, and thou shalt have treasure in heaven. . ." (Matt. 19:21)

Paul used perfect 17 times as descriptive of fitness for the kingdom of God. The root for the New Testament word "perfect" originates in the Old

Testament and is not limited to any particular book. God said to Abraham: "walk before me, and be thou perfect. . ." (Gen.17:1) Again Moses was commanded: "Thou shalt be perfect with the Lord. . ." (Deut. 18:31)

True understanding demands honesty. Manufactured evasions will never satisfy the claims of God's Word. The persistency of God's call from "uncleanness to holiness" is consistently the main stream running all the way through the scripture. Its presence is known; its demands felt; its meaning definite; its purpose is the ultimate for man's eternal salvation; its call clear; its scriptural understanding needs no further enlightenment, only to the prejudice mind.

To pursue the scriptural meaning of Christian Perfection, it will be necessary to determine the realm of perfection.

First, there is the realm of absolute perfection where there is absolutely no imperfection. That is only found in the Godhead. The Teleios used in the scriptural usage is referring to man, never seeking to seat man in absolute perfection, which would make him equal with God. The scripture is not trying to make us God, which would be contemptible and debasing.

Then, there is the realm where the Angels and Archangels exist. Every created creature who lives in God's presence must be holy, thus perfect after their kind. These angelic beings are perfect, yet have the freedom of choice. They are not machines driven by God. Those who chose to rebel were cast out their realm to their reward. These highly intelligent beings have chosen to live perfect in the realm in which God created them. But their perfection is not the Godhead perfection. God did not create them to be God.

Those angelic beings named Cherubims and Seraphims are also living in His presence, it appears there may be differences in at least responsibility, but they must be holy, perfect in their realm. They can only be perfect in their realm. They are not God nor are they men.

Another realm is the glorified saint. All who walk obediently in all the Light the Holy Spirit has shed on life's journey, and die in this obedience shall reign with Him, perfect in this glorified realm, not as God is absolutely perfect, nor as the angels are perfect in their realm. The perfection is only for ransomed redeemed saints. God did not create men to live above or below his realm, and his perfection must stay in this area for which his redemption has been purchased, and for which he was created.

Adam, in his original state was created perfect, without sin, innocent, perfect in the realm for which God created him. But he did not possess God's perfection, nor even the angels' perfection. He had a unique perfection all his own. God gave man an exceptional sphere in which no one but man was to move and live. Man is not responsible to any spectrum but his own. God has departmentalized His creation, and all created beings are held accountable only in their domain.

God requires perfection in one more realm, redeemed man. Christian perfection is the pinnacle of man's earthly salvation. God's redemptive plan and the depth to which He has gone to restore man says, "let us therefore, as many as be perfect be thus minded. . ." Follow closely, this perfection can only be obtained in our love for God. Perfect love has always been commanded: " Thou shalt love the Lord thy God with ALL. . ." That does not mean halfway, or ninety-nine per cent, but 100 per cent. God demands that perfect love, and will not accept second best. The Father's requirement has never been less, nor will it ever be less. To do so, would mean that we are not keeping the first commandment, the heart of obedience.

It was never the intention of the scripture to put man on God's level of perfection, nor any other heavenly being. Man is to have perfect love for God on his level just as the angels are have perfect love for God on their level. The scripture tells us the results of those angels that felt that perfect love and obedience was not necessary.

This can be illustrated by a circle that is one inch in diameter which can represent man's capacity. While a circle one foot in diameter will represent the angel's capacity. Each circle is 360 degrees, perfect, but with different capacities. Their variation of size does not limit their capacity to be perfect. Even each human being has different capacity for love, but whatever volume the individual soul has, requires a perfect love for God.

Bishop Reed explains Christian Perfection this way: "A little boy comes home from school, enthusiastically waves a report card, and shouts to his mother that he has received an 'A' in reading. What does this 'A' represent? Does it mean that he can read the essays of Emerson, or the Philosophy of William James? No! It means that he is a perfect reader in the third grade." (*Achieving Christian Perfection*, Bishop Reed, p. 12) He is accountable for third grade capacity, and he has lived up to that responsibility. God holds us answerable to live up to our potential, which is to love Him with ALL our hearts, which is perfect love.

AREAS OF LIMITATIONS!

Since we are particularly interested in man's realm, there are many areas of imperfection, because of our finiteness.

Consider man's judgment. No matter how perfect the love may be for God, he can still make wrong decisions. Without doubt the Christian who is led by the Holy Spirit will not make as many blunders as those who by-pass God's council. Judgmental errors are commonly used to discredit someone who takes a stand for Christian Perfection. I've never met anyone who claimed perfection in all decisions. There have been some board members who have come pretty close to that claim.

Consider the area of the intellect. Personally there are a number of things my intellect does not comprehend, and it is possible it never will. No matter how perfect our love for God, or how learned we are, we soon become aware that our capacities are very confined. No matter how great a mathematician, there is always the possibility of adding up a column of figures and getting the wrong answer, or over charging a customer and still have perfect love, if the motive was pure and there was no intention of fraud. Because of limited intellectual capacity we can make an honest mistake and still be living in perfect love. The intellect is not perfect, but the love can be.

Our God knows our boundaries and He also knows if there is deception, or if the motive is pure, and our Love for Him is ALL or divided. Our God doesn't play games, He deals with only eternal values. He will not diminish His holiness, to babble about whether He will agree with man, as to what kind of trash is acceptable. God doesn't deal in trash. If any are content with carnal trash, don't expect His blessing.

Consider physical imperfections. Depravity has left its mark, and death has entered into the human race. Our bodies give evidence of decay, and are subject to disease and infirmities. An individual may love God completely and be wholly deformed. Adam's fall left man with even greater limitations, this is seen in his creativity. Even though science has made enormous strides, there is no perfect machine. Thousands die because of man's failure to build a perfect machine. There are defects in everything man builds or creates. But in spite of all the inadequacy and imperfections, nothing can stand in the way of attaining perfect love, if there is enough mental capacity to understand His Truth.

There is no way anyone can walk away from the fact that our Lord has commanded us to be perfect in the realm of love for Him. "Be ye therefore perfect even as your Father in Heaven is perfect." Matt. 5:48. With this command must also come the possibilities of fulfillment or else God is a monster, who is demanding us do something He knows is impossible. "Faithful is he that calleth who will also do it." Now man is without excuse, Calvary has made the command achievable.

Jesus walking along the seashore came upon the sons of Zebedee mending their nets. They were perfecting their nets. Fishing nets are useless if there are holes in them. This comparison suggests that in order to be fully qualified for the Lord's service, all the rents the sinful nature has made in our lives must be spiritually perfected or we will be useless soul fishermen. If the inner life is not perfectly whole in our love for God, we will be guilty of allowing souls to slip through those carnal holes that refuse to surrender to the whole of God's will.

Christian perfection in a sense is allowing God the Father to mend and repair all the carnal nature has done to the soul, bringing the perfect love perfection God demands. This tense of repairing the division between God and man is always used with a view to perfect action.

Paul writing to the Corinthians gives his reason as: "we speak wisdom among the perfect. . ." (1 Cor. 2:6) This would remind them that there is a place of living for the Christian where he can know all the rents in the carnal nature have been repaired and he has experienced Christian adulthood. He is concerned that they be full-grown, of full age, and mature representatives of the Lord. Again, He put his thinking in these words to the Ephesians: "till we all come unto a perfect man. . ." (4:13) to the state of adults in Christ. Christ knows nothing of a holiness that does not manifest itself in outward and inward obedience to God and active service to man. The Apostle emphasizes this to the Philippians ". . .as many as be perfect. . ." arriving in experience to the mind of Christ and the character that verify this witness by the proper height of virtue and integrity in love for God and man.

Wherever Teleios is used it means completeness, arriving at the point of love perfection. It is wholeness and holiness in Christ – adulthood of virtue experienced and lived.

John Fletcher the great saint from out of the past defines Christian perfection in these words: "The pure love of God shed abroad in the heart by the Holy Ghost given unto us, to cleanse us and keep us clean from all filthiness of flesh and spirit, and to enable us to fulfill the law of Christ according to the talents we are entrusted with, the circumstance in which we are placed in the world."

Richard Hooker adds this thought that enlarges our discernment: "We count those things perfect which want nothing for the end where unto they were instituted."

In other words, if a man answers to the end for which he was created and designed, he is perfect. Man to please God by loving Him with all his heart is the only way God's purpose can be fulfilled. Man's full potential will never be reached, no matter what he achieves in life, if his love is not completely consummated in a holy and totally integrated relationship with the Trinity. Redeemed man can never reach in this life his spiritual summit as long as carnality inhibits access to God's best.

God never made man to be something he could not be in his realm. If an air conditioner unit was designed to adequately cool a room 20' X 30' but a purchaser thought he could place it in a building 100' X 100' and save the money the larger unit would cost, he would be greatly disappointed. When the workers felt no relief, he become very irritated with the manufacturer, and confronts them, charging that the air conditioner was useless. Why, was it worthless, because it wasn't designed for that big space? Take that same air conditioner and place it in a room for which it was designed and it will do the job perfectly.

God never calls his child to go or live beyond his capacity. As long as man is earthbound, he lives with limited capacity, but always has enough to fulfill God's command to love Him with all his heart and soul.

If we could put the world's most brilliant mind in control of this universe, what a calamity it would be. Can the imagination visualize this person recording the thoughts of 4 billion people all at once; numbering the number of hairs on the head of each person and have an up-to-date count at any minute in the day; making sure that every sparrow that falls from the sky is noted; keeping all the universe's objects in their proper orbit; regulating all temperatures of land, sea, and sky. This dear fellow would be beside himself in a few minutes time. He could be very efficient in managing the affairs of men, but totally incapable to oversee God's obligations. Why? He is out of his realm.

There are those who object to Christian perfection because they don't understand or refuse to understand. They try to make man more or less than what our God designed him to be. In many respects the Christian has many imperfections and these always glare at those who would like to disregard the requirements of Christian perfection. All is demanded from the lowly to those that consider themselves to be very important. Our God's whole passion is to have His people to be bond love slaves, for His glory.

Our calling is very personal, a perfection centered in love that is in proportion to the powers of each individual. Since there is no way to know what each person's capacity is, it can be used as an excuse for lowering any capacity to meet personal standards rather than God's standards. Man can fool others about his capacity, but not God. Our God is always aware of whether we are measuring up to the best He has for us.

Many professing Christians have already decided their capacity is very small. There is little or no exertion to enlarge their spiritual potential. This is the person that is in constant spiritual difficulty, because he is starving his soul by living too close to the famished border line. Look at the man Paul. He is pressing, and pressing again towards the mark of the high calling in Christ Jesus. Imagine him stopping near the initial beginning point. Loving God with all our hearts means, to the very limit of all our powers. When this is done, God will require no more. A glass of milk can be just as full as the gallon jug, neither one can hold more. No two individuals' love capacity is the same, but what capacity each one has is required to love God to full measure. Anything else in not acceptable.

SANCTIFICATION: A SECOND WORK OF GRACE AND ITS NECESSITY!

Look at what happened to the believers who tarried in the upper room after our Lord's ascension – "and they all filled with the Holy Ghost. . ." The Comforter is now the one who takes up His residence in each believer's heart that has surrendered all to Him. Now believers are seeing those who once lived in their defeats and fearfulness, but are now empowered by the Holy Spirit to risk life itself without apprehension or anxiety in the midst of animosity and hostility that was fermenting all around them, particularly in Jewish religious society.

What does the world need more than the purification of the inner nature that insists on ruling. The carnal carnage destroys every vestage of Spiritual growth and leaves the soul overtaken by his sensuous weaknesses. This only adds up to one Spiritual defeat after another. No one knows greater misery and distress than the one who wants to be holy, and finds within inner forces restricting the power to be what they know they should be. These glaring inconsistencies continue to reveal a shallowness that is embarrassing to anyone who is professing to be a sincere Christian. Any born again Christian who does not see the need for the carnal nature to be cleansed is not true to what they actually know about their personal inner life. Our God has gone on record to definitely state: "without holiness no man shall see the Lord." I don't know of any thing more concise.

Mr. Wesley replied to sanctification need in these words: "The more explicitly and strongly you press all believers to aspire after full sanctification, as attainable now by simple faith, the more the whole work of God will prosper."

It is the message that cannot be avoided, "be ye holy, for I am holy." Each Bible believing Christian is cognizant that this is not man given, but God commanded. None can escape its demand on each person's lifestyle. A watch would be useless if it didn't keep time; a gun that can't shoot straight is worthless; a banker that can't be trusted is insidious; leaving all at the mercy of that which will not function in the crisis hour. But God has not left us on life's mission with a faith that will not work in any of life's situations. He has given us life and eternity's answer.

Dr. J. D. Morrison explains sanctification to be the fulfillment of the inner demands of a true believer in these words: "When entire sanctification is come, then love becomes perfect. With hatred gone; and envy no more; and jealousy driven away, and pride cast out; and anger transformed; and malice removed; and unholy ambition sanctified, and self-seeking banished; and avarice nailed to the Cross; and covetousness clean gone forever; the heart, now released from its bondage to moral corruption swells with ecstasy of perfect love to God, perfect fellowship with God's children, and a tender compassion for the members of Adam's race."

Adulthood in the Christian's life will never be obtained outside sanctification, for it is the supreme end of God's redemptive appointed life. Here is the crown and ornament of all other graces, the perfecting of moral virtue. The fact that God calls each person, He then believes, each one is capable of personal holiness, which indicates its necessity.

Anyone knowingly living beneath the privilege of a pure heart is not ready for eternity. Just circumventing the fact of death will not make it less certain. A certain millionaire forbade the word "death" to be used in his presence. He was known to have run people out of his house when they mentioned "death." Evidently he operated on the principle he could confidently avoid its fixed place in life, if he could get it out of his mind. Certain facts are incontestable no matter what is done to escape them.

Many stumble over their perceived ideas of what they want from God, rather than what the Father wants to give them. Since they want only what they want, and not what God gives, they will remain empty, struggling to survive spiritually. If true victory is ever going to be obtained, it will be God's way or not at all.

WHAT DOES IT MEAN TO BE SANCTIFIED?

M. W. Knapp said it best this way:

"It does not exempt from temptation, but gives victory over it. It does not make absolutely perfect, but perfect in love. It does not eliminate humanity, but carnality. It does not destroy free agency, making man a machine, but causes him to gladly choose the whole will of God. It does not exempt from mistakes, sins of ignorance, but from inbred sin and sinning against light. It does not give a perfect head, but a pure heart full of perfect love. It does not enable its possessor to walk above human criticism, misunderstanding, and persecution, but gives no just occasion for these things. It does not exempt from slander, but gives victory over it. It does not make us oblivious to insults, but fully saves amid them. It does not insure from the possibility of falling into sin, but makes this far less probable. It does not give "freedom" to disregard the Word of God, the Spirit of God, or the Son of God, but makes their triple leadership a delight. It does not make one perfect in human eyes, but in God's sight."

"Sanctification does cleanse the heart from all sin. It does impart perfect love, which casteth out all slavish fear of man, of foes, of death, of hell, and of the judgment. It does make "dead indeed unto sin and alive unto God." It does fill with the Holy Ghost. It does make more than conquerors. It does eliminate all irritability, evil tempers, murmurings, fretting, and repining. It does so destroy the "old man" of sin, and "cast him out" of the heart that his motions are no more felt. It does eliminate the "bear," and the snapping "turtles" and the "peacock," and replace with the lamb, the lily, and the dove. It does eliminate stinginess, and crown liberality."

WHAT JUSTIFICATION DOES, IN CONTRAST TO WHAT SANCTIFICATION IS!

Justification pardons,.	Sanctification gives heart purity.
Justification makes right,	Sanctification makes blameless.
Justification removes guilt,	Sanctification removes pollution.
Justification represses carnality,	Sanctification purges carnality.
Justification gives desire to please God,	Sanctification makes this possible.
Justification enters us into God's kingdom,	Sanctification establishes in His kingdom.
Justification brings forgiveness,	Sanctification gives the holy heart.
Justification awakens Spiritual sensitivities,	Sanctification purifies the senses.

In Sanctification there can not be any mixture that could tarnish the soul. The holiness our God demand's that no shame or reproach be a part of our baggage. That which can defile, the sanctified life rejects wholeheartedly. Sanctification gives a consistently godly lifestyle. Sanctification can never be obtained if unbelief is present, or the refusal to allow self to be crucified, or if the fear of the unknown is a factor in the decision, or if there is a lack of determined will, to will God's will only. Sanctification is more than a bombastic and superfluous wheezily pumped up emotional excitement, it is the peace and tranquility that rests in the soul when passing through life's darkest hours. Sanctification is that which can disagree without being disagreeable; the ability to abstain from the questionable without exhibiting a haughty arrogance; the discipline to be reasonable and sensitive, when others lose control; the discernment to not exploit this doctrine by over stating perfect love by taking positions that will sidetrack from its truth, but make sure all is Bible centered.

Rev. George Ridout describes sanctifying grace as: "It is that grace by which the soul comes into possession of faith like Abraham, patience like Job, hope like Moses, perseverance like Noah, meekness like David, temperance like Daniel, prayerfulness like Elijah, unworldliness like James, holiness like Peter, love like John, guilelessness like Nathaniel, devotion to God and to Jesus like Paul. It is that grace which will let you sing in trial like Paul and Silas, help you to be prayed out of prison like Peter, keep you in the hottest fire of affliction like the three Hebrew children. Sanctification is super-nature power to arrest, to control, to destroy. Sanctification is an habitual grace. Holiness becomes a habit on earth; here the saints do on earth as they do in Heaven." (*The Beauty of Holiness*, George W. Ridout, D.D. p. 3 & 4)

Martin Luther has said: "The Holiness of common Christianity is this: that the Holy Spirit gives the people faith in Christ and sanctifies them thereby; that is, makes a new heart, soul, body, work, and being and writes the law of God, not on tables of stone, but in fleshly hearts. He sanctifies them, not only by forgiveness of sin, but also by the laying aside, expelling and destroying sin."

Sanctification cleanses the nature that allows man to completely identify with the will of God. Consecration and full surrender, man's part, must precede the definite act of personal sanctification. Which is God's part. This positions the soul to embrace the Father's will in life's most unpleasant and difficult situations. Brengle, that great saint of God, dictated these moving words to his wife during one of his most serious illnesses: "I think there is a noble. . .majesty in pain. It is pleasure strung to concert pitch. A great musician can discover harmonies where an ordinary fellow could hear only discords: and I seem to sense that there is, somehow or somewhere, to be discovered a great harmony in pain." (*The Brick and the Book*, by Eric Coward, p. 15)

It is the joy of every good man to know he is good by possessing a witness to his goodness in his Spirit lightened conscience. The joy deepens by knowing his goodness is not his own, for he had none, but by a divine miraculous gift of God through the agency of the Holy Spirit. Why, because man's goodness can only come from the imparting of God's purity.

All major orthodox denominations have a position in their book of discipline which further exhibits its scriptural position and necessity. John Wesley the father of Methodism writes in his "A Plain Account of Christian Perfection" on page 15 & 16 these questions and answers:

Q. "What is Christian Perfection?"

A. "The loving God with all our heart, mind, soul and strength. This implies that no wrong temper, none contrary to love, remains in the soul; and that all the thoughts, words and actions are governed by pure love."

Q. "Do you affirm that this perfection excludes all infirmities, ignorance and mistakes?"

A. "I continually affirm quite the contrary, and always have done so."

Q. "But how can every word and work be governed by pure love, and the man be subject at the same time to ignorance and mistake?"

A. "I see no contradiction here. A man may be filled with pure love, and still be liable to mistake. Indeed, I do not expect to be freed from actual mistake till this mortal puts on immorality. I believe this to be a natural consequence of the soul's dwelling in flesh and blood. . .And hence we cannot avoid sometimes thinking wrong till this corruptible shall have put on incorruption. . ."

WHAT SANCTIFICATION IS NOT!

Sanctification is not the two nature theory popularized by those who needed to explain the carnality they still retain. The two nature theory states that the depraved nature received at birth will be possessed while earthbound, and there isn't anything that can be done with it but suppress it.

Even God is without a remedy. This theory maintains when an individual is justified, he receives a new nature which will co-exist side by side with the old nature. If the professing Christian willfully sins, it is the old nature. The new nature is entirely pure, bathed in Christ's imputed righteousness, while the old nature still retained, is carnal, mean and enmity against God. When once one of these natures is obtained, neither can be put off in this life. They are always the believer's whether you want them or not. But the raging conflict the two engage will continue in great intensity until physical death, then the old will perish and the new live on.

This convenient theory is substituted for the Act of Sanctification where by the Holy Spirit cleanses the old nature so it is removed and the self life and enmity against God is crucified.

Sanctification is not sinless perfection in all phases of life. Perfection is only claimed in MOTIVE. This needs to be understood. A Christian when justified is saved from sin, and does not commit willful, known sin, even before the act of sanctification. But there is a necessity to deal with the carnal nature that explodes unwillingly. Sanctification deals with this nature, but that does not mean any person will live a faultless life. All who are sanctified are subject to wrong judgments, (not willful), will make mistakes because of this; that can appear to be sin in the eyes of others through ignorance because LIGHT has not been given on that particular thing or situation. If motive is pure, even though the appearance is otherwise, the heart is pure and holy in God's sight. God always looks at the motive, not the act, even when the act can be plain stupidity. Our limitations will always be with us and serve to be burdensome, but they must not interfere with the pureness of our motives.

SANCTIFICATION DOES NOT MEAN IT IS IMPOSSIBLE FOR ONE TO SIN.

Dr. H. C. Morrison once said in referring to this question: "God has not fixed me up so that I can't sin if I want to, but He has fixed me up so that I can't sin and enjoy it any more." The soul is replaced from the want to, to the I don't have a taste for that garbage any more. Why go back to the vomit and the wallow? The pleasure of sins are replaced by the willingness to be a door keeper in the house of the Lord, and becoming a servant rather than being served. The disposition to sin has been removed, but the possibility is there. But man must be free to choose. If not, the Savior would never have known the joy of man's willing obedience, or the love that man freely gives to the God who loved and redeemed him. For the Father to see the crown of His creation be "more than conquerors" delights His soul. He revels in man's victory over his worst enemy. As man has his greatest joy in his intimate relationship with the Savior, so the Savior has His satisfaction and pleasure in enjoying the peace and rest He gives the inner man. especially in life's most bitter hour.

Then, think it not strange that it delights our Savior to take his child by the hand when he walks through the valley of the shadow of death. Yes, it is possible for a Sanctified soul to go back into sin, but who would want to exchange that blessed hope for anything this world has to offer. Temptation will still be knocking at the Sanctified soul's door, and as long as there is life, there will be choices to be made, but he lives in a Grace that is adequate for each temptation. Adam's pure heart was corrupted when temptation entered life's arena. With all his purity and perfection, he made the wrong choice. The possibility is always there, but so is the Grace for victory.

FANATICISM IS NOT BIBLICAL SANCTIFICATION!

Sanctification is wholeness, balance, harmony, and completeness. Fanaticism rests on wanting to wield his own flicking torch and fancy's it is spirit inspired. He scorns fact and reason to fit personally into his creative imagination so he no longer needs direction, but lives by his impulse and whims. This person can consider himself to be faultless and can never make a mistake, which brings endless reproach on Holiness. Human limitations make error unavoidable.

CHRISTIAN PERFECTION IS NOT ABSOLUTE PERFECTION.

Only the Godhead has absolute perfection. The angels' perfection is not absolute, nor is man's. Christian perfection does not give a special protective shield against bitter disappointments, sorrows, broken hearts or burdensome anguish. (2 Co. 1:8). It rests on the first commandment: "Thou shalt love the Lord thy God with ALL thy heart, with ALL thy soul, and with ALL thy mind." (Matt. 22:37). This is perfect love or Christian perfection. Again, I state that perfect love is only realized in the realm of that whole love for God, and man.

SANCTIFICATION IS NOT SUPPRESSION, NOR IS IT ENACTED AT THE POINT OF PHYSICAL DEATH.

There are those who know without holiness no man can see God, to remedy this, those who reject it have found an escape in teaching, that at death sanctification is engaged at that point. But there is nowhere that the scripture teaches that death has any redemptive power. God only acts when an active rational mind approaches the throne with a trusting faith, thus, meeting God's conditions. Death is not meeting God's conditions. Yes, there is a possibility of deathbed repentance, but any business done with God must be done with a rational mind before death takes place.

SANCTIFICATION IS NOT MATURITY.

Sanctification is an instantaneous act by the Holy Spirit the moment a wholly yielded faith touches heaven's throne. It is at this point maturity and real growth start. No one grows into Holiness, they receive holiness or sanctification at a definite time and then that which did not allow a holy heart is gone, and the road is clear of the besetting carnality. With this done, maturity in the fullest sense of the word, starts. Maturity will be dealt with as the next step.

SANCTIFICATION DOES NOT REMOVE THE NATURAL GOD GIVEN DRIVES.

There is nothing in Sanctification that does away with God given drives. The Holy Spirit only cleanses and controls them to glorify the Lord who gave them. This part of humanity is surrendered to be kept in the bounds of holy living. Anything less, these drives will create havoc and downfall that will bring shame to God and man. Sanctification does not dehumanize anyone. Man receives an imparted holiness from God, but is still very much a human being. We still get hungry, but that does not permit gluttony; sex is not sin, but must be kept in scriptural marriage relationship, but adultery is sin; disliking an individual and what they do is not sin, but hating the person is; wanting something is not sin, but coveting is. All passions and appetites must be controlled by the Holy Spirit, that does not leave us without responsibility for personal disciplines necessary to place them at all times under the Holy Spirit's authority.

SANCTIFICATION IS NOT SELF RIGHTEOUSNESS.

Sanctification is a life to be lived in the freedom of the Spirit, not some morbid cold dish full of legalism that has no responsive Spirit. Sanctification is not a rotten decaying out-moded set of rules, the holy life style has built within it, characteristics exemplary for holy healthy everyday living. This way of life has a potency and vitality that can not only revolutionize the individual, but whole societies have been transformed which history has documented. These movements were not resurrected by arrogant haughty self centered prudes, but by holy servants laying their daily lives on the line, for the Lord and the lost masses. People were caught by their passionate love for God and man, because God's Spirit is witnessing through them. The fire once lit in their souls torches others.

There must be a lowly mind as in Christ Jesus, clothed in holy humility, with the willingness to give the benefit of the doubt to others, even as you want them to do to you. We do not humiliate weaknesses, nor excuse or disguise them, but realize all are faulty, and what we see is not necessarily what God sees. Why, because I'm sure they are aware of ours. But again, purity of motive is what God sees. Christian perfection shines through the simplicity of a childlike faith when faults are recognized, and exposed. When the Spirit calls to our attention what appears to be a broken promise, but in reality it was a forgotten promise, do we allow ourselves this kind of charity? Quite a difference! Isn't it good God knows the motive, while we know only the appearance. Holy love will always overshadow faults with a prayerful understanding, others will love you in spite of your faults. Of course, the self-righteous have no faults.

SANCTIFICATION IS NOT A COMMON MOLD.

God made each one as a very distinct individual, even though we all must come through and by His plan for our salvation; He still deals with us as a unique individual in the salvation walk Because there are varied personalities, temperaments, drives, and dispositions; these create diverse problems that call for discrete exclusive attention. Only God knows the particular Light each person needs to lead them in holy living. This is a source of difficulty in the church, the saints want to fit every one into their personal mold. But they may not have the same Light you have. It could be, they need more Light, but it will take far more Grace to pray for them than to criticize. More people than we know are defeated, because there were those who were pushed in an area where Spiritually they are not prepared to go. This kind of pushing can overwhelm and discourage. Handle gently and with holy care. This is a unique precious child of God. Don't cram and stuff. Lead with a holy life and godly instruction from His Word, feed patiently, understand when you don't understand; care when it appears to be useless. Eternity is involved and the result may rest with you and the church. Walk softly, for a priceless unperishable soul is at risk.

SANCTIFICATION IS NOT AN UNBALANCED LIFE.

There is no way an unbalanced life can be associated with a truly Sanctified life. Wholeness, completeness and purity is balance. Jesus condemned the unbalanced life of the Pharisees. They displayed punctiliously the tithing of bits and pieces of "mint, anise, and cummin," but neglecting such plain, obvious responsibilities as "judgment, mercy and faith." Jesus exposes these barren lives for what they were. They should pay their tithes, but they must also exhibit holy judgment, mercy and faith. It is evident that an unbalanced life can become a rationalized life, where halfway is good enough. There are multitudes at the point in their Spiritual lives putting on a religious front, but allowing a seared conscience to discriminate in what is necessary for holy living and what is personally advantageous. This has never been acceptable to the Lord, nor will it ever be. Nothing can poison the inner life more than trying to portray holiness, when it is not possessed.

Only the Lord knows the number that retain bitterness, resentment and unforgiveness but still carry on a religious front, performing all the duties of sainthood. How contemptible and hypocritical! This throws the whole spiritual mechanism out of balance, leaving the soul mastered by that which is the seed of sure doom. An unbalanced flywheel put in motion will destroy itself.

SANCTIFICATION IS NOT SOLELY EXTERNAL, BUT. . .

True, in the past, some holiness people put great emphasis on the external, but now the pendulum has plunged in the opposite direction. The fickleness of mankind can not get it right, that includes spiritual people. They jump from one extreme to another. I am shocked by the way people dress to come into God's house, a strip joint doesn't have too much more to offer. This is overstated somewhat, but the ridiculous way some come to God's house is embarrassing to others, if not to themselves. It is difficult to grasp their concept of the holy God, and what righteousness and holiness means to them. Evidently it is no more than a daily perception of common acceptability in their worldly surroundings. Does not this reveal an inner disregard for anything more than the sleazy lifestyle accepted as normal? What a shabby demonstration for all that is supposed be righteous and holy.

Music, if you want to call it music, is almost sacrilege. A retired minister and I were walking into the sanctuary on our way to the morning prayer meeting, and the choir was practicing. He said: "I thought for a moment I was in Hank's bar." So much of its rhythm seems to loom out of the darkness of a satanic drum beat that whips its worshipers into a frenzied dance. Sanctified music doesn't forget who God is. Our God is the God of dignity, virtuous and awesome in His sacred excellence, which does not allow us to bring God down and mire Him our subculture and its slime. This is not meant to be prudish, or suggest that our music should be a funeral dirge. There is nothing more deadening to a service than slow, drawn out hymns. The gospel has spiritual life that is joyously honoring the God of all joy, but that is because He lifts us, we are not dragging Him down to our sludge. So much of this type of music has no depth, or theology, nothing more than repetition of a few words that is sought to fan the emotions. Sanctification is far more than appearance and music, but it is also wrapped up in that which is to glorify God only in these areas.

SANCTIFICATION IS NOT EXCESSIVE CLAIMS.

It is necessary we give room for human limitations. This is the world in which we live whether we like it or not. Sensitive souls are defeated if human limitations are pushed beyond their reality. Some, particularly in the past, have thrust Sanctification almost to the point of absolute perfection, and when the limitations of reality have set in, their faith has been shattered, at least severely crippled. They found out they could be aggravated, incensed and provoked to the point of losing it, that circumstances are not perfect in an imperfect world. They have suddenly become aware that life is not always calm, sweet, and poised. Is God's wrath carnal? Never! Righteous wrath demands righteousness bathed in purity. All Sanctified wrath must be likewise. Wrath must be centered upon that which the Bible views as unrighteous, when it is otherwise, it becomes sinful. There is a vast difference between faultlessness and blamelessness, our limitations must realize that, and not try or seek a perfection that was never intended.

SANCTIFICATION IS NOT AN OPTION.

Accountability does not give options as far as God is concerned. Spiritual Light demands obedience, or willful disobedience. Once the Holy Spirit reveals carnality for what it is, there is no way this Biblical truth can be excused. No matter what the doctrinal background, there is no escape, just because your group did not think a clean pure nature was a necessity. It will always be true, "without Holiness no man shall see God." Our God isn't about to change it just because someone did not think it necessary.

SANCTIFICATION IS NOT GRADUAL.

What a number have advocated is, you just grow and grow and eventually you will arrive. When? How do you know when you are fully and wholly Sanctified? What these, some most sincere, are trying to do is, grow and reap something that has never been planted. There may be a growth of knowledge and light as to the need that is evident in the inner life, but that only brings the soul to the point where his God is sought with all the heart. This conviction brings the soul face to face with the demand for a clean and holy heart. There must be a definite time when the Holy Spirit cleansed the carnal nature, and you know He has. This is a crisis experience. At this exact time, God planted the Sanctified seed which now can grow because the weeds carnality produces have been removed. There must be a time when this work has been done, and it will be known to the surrendered heart. No guess work is involved, hoping and guessing will not stand the test at the judgment.

PITFALLS POSSIBLE IN THE SANCTIFIED LIFE.

Without doubt, at the top of the list is defective and unsound scriptural teaching. On the whole most people do not like to think. It is probably because it is easier not to think deeply, than to do it. It is the custom these days to let others do the thinking and then hand their thoughts over because the masses are too busy with that which takes little thought, to spend the time thinking about the riches of eternity that are at hand, and needed to fulfill the emptiness of the soul. But this lack of understanding is the shroud that breeds bewilderment and doubts. Too often there is confusion because the heart and head are not at one. The conflict rages within and the battle leaves the wounded bleeding, too many times with no one to bind and care for the disheartened.

There are always those who carry the air of piety, but inconsistent living betrays true holiness leaving the multitudes to judge the sanctified life by what they are seeing lived before them. They judge by Biblical standards, by which they refuse to live, resulting in prejudices and warped perceived ideas. Whenever self is at the heart of action, the Holy Spirit is grieved beyond measure. This always leads to a side track where various self made perceptions leads to further fallacies. No one can dare to under estimate personal influence.

One of the most obvious and subtle pitfalls is to be satisfied with the nominal. There is no pressing towards the mark of the high calling in Christ Jesus. These anchor themselves as close to the border of the forbidden as they dare, and still declare full victory. If there is one thing the Sanctified life does, it is to destroy mediocrity. Our God demands our talents be increased daily. Token intensity is a mere whitewash which victimizes its deceived captive.

A sure pitfall is the lack or neglect of a devotional life that leaves barren all other aspects of the Spiritual life, including soul winning. There is always a direct relationship between a man's prayer life and Bible study, and a personal concern for the lost. Prayerless souls have little desire to see others brought to the Savior. If there is insignificant time to study God's Word and have an earnest and vital prayer life, another's spiritual condition will matter little.

Some have fallen by the wayside simply because they have been led to believe that anyone who professes sanctification is self-righteous. This lack of confessing and standing for its truth, grieves the Holy Spirit. This constant neglect assures defeat and backsliding, leaving the soul drained of its spiritual strength.

Fanaticism drops the soul into almost an irretrievable pit, because usually there is meaningless logic with baseless scriptural consistency. No believer doubts that there needs to be fixed convictions, as an absolute necessity on Biblical doctrines, but not on the trivial, such as the mode of water baptism. Usually the trivial are the result of being unsure of the position taken, it then becomes necessary to go overboard to convince self, meanwhile losing personal status and the influence wanted, but never achieved.

WHAT SANCTIFICATION SHOULD DO FOR US!

Sanctification is the dominant experience in the believer's life if he is going to have Spiritual victory now. In this experience is our God's redemptive plan fully stipulated. Our God gives this work of Grace the crowning experience needed, perfecting every moral virtue of man's nature. Sanctification is implemented to bring man to the preeminent place for which our God made man, fully restored to please his Creator and to mature in his spiritual walk

The whole man is activated to serve as a servant wherever the Lord may chose; which includes his intellectual capacities; his spiritual resources; his physical assets; his concerns and plans; and his will to do God's will. The sanctified man has experienced wholeness. Holiness is undivided completeness to serve the Master with every measure of strength and being. God's man is not lopsided, off centered because he is centered, focused on the prize of the high calling of God in Christ Jesus. His one desire is to enlarge his spiritual capacity so he can better serve his Lord.

Scriptural Holiness means fitness to lead others into this holy walk; to fire the hearts of the lukewarm; consistently traveling the narrow high road, ever discerning the enemy's road blocks; watchfully guarding and warning fellow travels of the deceptive curves that would derail the unsuspected; being worthy soldiers to carry our Lord's blood stained banner. No matter how difficult the task, there is the constant awareness that the labor is not in vain. God's highest and best is never useless, but rather the partaker can expect miracles in areas where defeat ruled before. Our God has much to give, sanctified man is in the right position to receive these glorious benefits.

The act is done, the Holy Spirit's gift is given, and every motive has Christ's call in mind. This abounding love incites actions, and arouses a genuine forgiveness towards those who misunderstand; hatred will receive love in return; contempt is replaced by understanding; disdain for Holiness is covered by compassion.

The God of glory becomes and is the sole governor. Thus, the enemy is conquered, and assurance is possessed. Circumstances are not allowed to control the motive. There is a consciousness that nothing can separate us from God's love, but our willfulness. Romans 8:28 takes over these situations. There comes this bond of perfect confidence, that God is no respecter of person but is always just, merciful, and righteous in all His decisions and what He allows to come upon us. Everything that arrives on our doorstep, is not there because God put it there, but in the unwanted, He can give the certainty that all is in His control. This is renewed reassurance that the Father is caring for His own regardless of the dilemma on hand.

The undisciplined areas are sanctified, and brought under spiritual mastery. Unwelcome conditions are not only endured, but there is an awareness that the Father is fashioning a masterpiece out of such an unworthy lump of clay. The disciplined schooling comes from life's trials which are now accepted as a part of God's molding process. There is meaning for His child in every heartache. God's schooling is never without a laborious cross. Harsh tasks only sharpen the spiritual edge for more discerning comprehension of the Father's plan.

Furthermore, menial chores are a check on what is happening to the ego or pride that raise its ugly head at any moment. The sanctified will soon find how sanctified they are if asked to minister in a subservient roll, rather than to be ministered to. Is it difficult to remember all is in His hands? His care takes us through life's darkest valley and lights the pathway with His presence.

The disposition of the sanctified man has much to do with his witness and influence. Our spirit creates an atmosphere, just as God's Spirit, or the Devil's spirit. Our spirit invokes a climate, whether it is the workplace or the home. Notice how some people's presence changes the conditions of the area from an ugly, mean situation to a kind, gentle setting. A thankful spirit must be cultivated each day. The spirit must be disciplined as well as the mind and will. Depression and despair can be tilled without too much effort. A grateful spirit must have even more attention because it will defeat depression. The Psalmist understood how praise and thankfulness could raise the soul to the highest mountain from the deepest valley.

A great revealing and rewarding transformation hits the pocketbook when the carnal man is crucified and the sanctified man takes over. The tithe is a minimum. Jesus said this ought ye to have done. The love offerings exceed the tithe. Godly compassion is always bathed in sacrificial sharing; thriftiness goes with generosity; frugal but benevolent; economical but abundantly charitable. This soul is in perfect condition for growth.

I have no idea where I found this article. I had written on it, from an English writer, but truth can leap across oceans. Should we not allow this God inspired man to speak even if he is unknown, for in a few words he sums up what sanctification should do for the sanctified.

"(1) A holy prayerfulness, deep and yearning. (2) A loving, joyful, peaceful, trustworthy, meek, self-controlled walk in human life. (3) A tendency toward a holy union with other children of God as will not be obstructed by the life and spirit of self. (4) A joy and delight in adoration and generally in being at the will and service of the adored Lord. (5) A deepening consciousness of the truth conquering power of the Word of God as the sword in the spiritual combat. (6) A growing gladness in the experience of a meek and lowly but most real sacrifice and surrender in all things to God. (7) A quiet readiness to be led by the Spirit and that leading will always be out of the way and will of self into that of God. (8) A larger insight into what is meant by a life of faith, a life of unreserved reliance on the promises and will of God, a reliance ever more childlike in its simplicity and ever more mature and strong and prevailing in its results. (9) Deliverance from serving sin. that so we may be filled with his "calm exceeds" and may overflow for blessing in the around. (10) The man born of the Spirit, led of the Spirit, taking step by step by the Spirit, filled with this same blessed Spirit lives, moves, and has his being with, and for, God and man. Well may we close this sketch with the deep and soulful hymn of Gregory the Great:"

"Come, Holy Ghost, our souls inspire,
And lighten with celestial fire;
Thou the anointing Spirit art,
Who dost thy sevenfold gifts impart;
Thy blessed unction from above

Is comfort, life, and fire of love.

"Enable with perpetual light
The dullness of our blinded sight;
Anoint and cheer our soiled face
With the abundance of thy grace;
Keep far our foes, give peace at home;
Where thou art guide, no ill can come."

WITNESSING TO THE EXPERIENCE OF SANCTIFICATION IS A PART OF HISTORY.

A personal experience is the best evidence God can give man as to the reality of this actual Spiritual experience. Ridicule, unbelief filled with Gnosticism and skepticism has used a host of brilliant minds to try and bury this truth forever, but here it is, in the hearts of mankind to outlive its bitter foes. Torture nor death itself, has not silenced their voices. Personal experience imparted by the Holy Spirit, supersedes reason, as will all God's virtues.

I could trot out a great host who could witness to this marvelous experience, but as always, if the heart and mind is set in disbelief, no matter how many are paraded before the prejudiced carnal mind, it will never yield.

What is man without God's power? What is man without a clean heart? Everything within seeks purity from the uncleanness. All mankind cries out to be righteousness. There is no peace or satisfaction without the nature's inner cleansing. Who would dare to set limits on God and what He can do and wants to do in individuals' lives. His question to Sarah will suffice: "Is anything impossible with God?" Can anyone imagine how dangerous it is to put limits on the Living God?

Oh, blessed walk! Let every privilege be accompanied by obedience. Arise transformed soul, claim your inheritance. Walk where holy men have walked; drink from the cup out of which He drank; eat of the bread that has satisfied the multitudes through the ages; pray in the anguish that crushed Him in the garden; climb Calvary's hill with His cross on your back; there you can rightfully commend your spirit, soul, and body to the Father for use as He sees fit; now the tomb can be entered in confidence – He is there. Only the pure of heart can claim that!

One Bishop of early Methodism when dying said, "Oh, Christian perfection, Oh, perfect love, Oh, sanctification. It is heaven on earth to be sanctified wholly. This experience fits you for both worlds."

What is the route this multitude has taken? It is a simple trail. FAITH, the childlike obedience that refuses to allow unanswerable questions stand in the way of the Faith that will leads to total Spiritual victory. Abraham had such a faith that was unquestionable when he surrendered Isaac on the altar on that mountaintop. There was no question who was first in Abraham's life. His reckless Faith abandoned all reason, being careful for nothing. We stand in the shadow of such Faith exhibited, for there was no adversary adequate to terrorize the simplicity of his trust. This type of Faith arouses God to action.

As stated before we have at hand a considerable number such as: Ignatuis, Bishop of Antioch, Irenuis, Marcarius, the Wesleys, Asbury, Bringle, Sangster, Steele, Muller, Chadwick, D. L. Moody, and the endless list, who have witnessed to this glorious Grace. Space will not allow their personal witness, but their works stand as a monument of this scriptural experience that all need to claim.

CHAPTER X

MATURITY

What is maturity and its importance?

When the act of sanctification is a personal reality, so many are of the opinion that they have arrived. But the truth is, for the first time they are in the position to actually begin this holy walk. Too many are like the two ladies who approached the golf pro, who said: "do you want to learn how to play the game of golf?" One replied: "No, but my friend does, I learned yesterday."

The maturing walk with the Father is a life-long experience. The closer our walk the more unworthy we feel. This faithful awareness will continually reveal that we can do nothing of real worth without Him who gives everything that has value more value. There is a real understanding of just how inadequate we are in ourselves. It further establishes just how much He is needed to give life its true purpose. He is now our sole source.

Maturity is the beginning of understanding how thoroughly necessary it is to rest in Him to work out our everyday situations. Meaning of course, that He is our governor, and we must possess no will but His will. It is all "to serve the present age, His calling to fulfill." This journey is filled with continual daily choices that involves personal obedience in the midst of a life that has ever-changing circumstances. Adjustments are necessary to bring the will of God into harmony with these situations. This utter surrender to all the fluctuating events is to bring the totality of life into realization of God's best. Our holy God is the object of all personal love which engenders a greater expectation of His fellowship. This can only make the child of God more aware of personal weaknesses and inadequacies. This intimate walk more clearly reveals how insecure this tangible world is, and how imperative it is to cling to the solid rock, Christ Jesus.

The maturing person is determined as was Paul "not to know anything among you, save Jesus Christ and Him crucified." (1 Cor. 2:2) Oswald Chambers in his book *Philosophy of Sin* says: "How much more is there to know for instance after Sanctification? Everything! Before Sanctification, we know nothing, we are simply put in the place of knowing; that is, we are led up to the Cross; in Sanctification we led through the Cross – for what purpose? For a life of outpouring service to God." (p. 17)

How dare we relax to review what was recorded as past accomplishments, lest we linger to think of Egypt and the garlic and onions. It is always onward and upward. The danger of Spiritual weariness is on every side, but no attainment has "finish" written on it, for there is always the possibility of progress. This is the way God is. God being eternal, there is always a ceaseless progress which knows no end, for is not our God without end?

The soul is in an observatory viewing the endless horizons, discovering new stars and galaxies; taking the soul to new heights, but this takes time. The reason there are so few saints that qualify for the meaning of the term, is because it takes time to get behind the telescope to view the teachable wonders that make God, God. Believers live in a presser keg, ready to explode with today's schedule. The alarm goes off, then the necessities before flight to the demands for the day, grasping a banana on the way out the door; then the mad pursuit of goal two, beat the traffic. After dodging the maniac drivers; arriving at the job, the reason, only to put bread and butter on the table. The day is filled with a grumbling slothful attitude that one's worth is not being appreciated. Again that traffic, home at last, but the evening appointment demands a shower and clothes change, a quick bite, and out the door. Later the garage door is shut, and the key unlocks the back door, too weary to even look in the refrigerator, the next flop hit the bed. Of course, each day is the same. Do you see sainthood sprouting from that routine? But it does keep a roof overhead and food on the table, and that is about all. No time to grow Spiritually, which is the only possession that will go with you when standing in His presence to give an account of all of life.

Growing pains should be one of the happenings in the maturing life. Ambitions will be God-centered and vitalized; capacities will be enlarged;

holy zeal cannot be extinguished; forgiving love will endure. This soldier of the cross will never flee the battle's front line and when others would falter, he refuses defeat.

This victorious soul takes on wings and soars above the ugly circumstance and reaches for new pinnacles to expand the whole inner man in faith's intangibles. Discouragement will not allow dismay; opposition cannot prevail; adversities are only momentarily obstacles; affliction is a cross bearing conquest; distress has triumph already written on it; fear is mastered by His Grace; hope overshadows despair, with victory placed in our hand.

Maturity is always in pursuit of Spiritual excellence. It refuses to drop into legalism or pharisaism by walking in scriptural Light. It avoids conforming to man-made rules, but seeks a higher law, invoked by the living God. There is a continual realization that our full conformity is to the Master's will if there is to be that continual Spiritual growth. Spiritual growth is at the heart of maturity – no growth, no maturity.

What is healthy growth? It is constant God fullness. Its fullness cannot be contained, so it grows, to accommodate more, and keeps doing so as long as physical breath is given. Is this growth earth bonded? I believe not! Anything of God and eternity has an endlessness to it. What God has made, has unending growth. It cannot die, for God made us in His image. There is a plant in South America that is called the "pitcher plant." That pitcher-like formation holds water all the time, whether it is small or large, it is filled with water. No matter what its capacity, the pitcher is always full. Is not that what God's maturing child should be, always full of His Spirit, whether the capacity is small or large? Our God never made anything stagnate. It is stench to His nostrils. Can we not expect the angels to have growth in the unalterable law that is universally embedded in the fiber of the universe?

This maturing growth must exhibit itself in every nook and cranny of our lives, whether it is gratitude, thanksgiving, praise, fasting, prayer, compassion, soul winning, or holy love for God and man. These attitudes and approaches to life need to reflect Spiritual growth. The scripture entreats us to do all things in the name of the Lord Jesus Christ, giving thanks unto God and the Father by Him. Our fullness of His presence is an automatic response to His Goodness.

Phillips translates Colossians 2:7 this way: "Grow out of Him as a plant out of the soil it is planted in, becoming more and more sure of your ground, and your lives will overflow with joy and thankfulness." Like any good grace, thankfulness must be cultivated to grow. When our God is exalted, all other graces will grow accordingly. Wesley felt grace was more difficult to "retain" than to "gain." Retaining demands constant vigilance, gaining is for the moment. Retaining equals spiritual growth; spiritual increase mandates cross-bearing; cross-bearing indicates sacrifice; sacrifice stipulates forfeiting personal rights and privileges; but spiritual gain is not without renouncing the good for the best. Personal satisfaction with the good can never retain the best our Lord wants us to possess.

But the whole process of retaining maturing spiritual grow, is caught in the web of our easy lifestyle. For years at our home for boys, we needed godly middle age couples to help. An age of 40 and older was important, so teenagers could have a father and mother image. But we had only one taker, they only stayed a short time. The pressures were too much. They did not have to take the daily hustle that these kind of young fellows dished out. First, it was a faith work, where some received no salary and others a small one. That is never appetizing. Second, it was 24 hours a day that ears and eyes needed to be on the alert. Thirdly, most at that age were in the process of purchasing a home and getting things together for retirement. Fourth, there was the salary and the pension plan that was considered to be their security. Now what fool would want to leave that and be without possibilities of having anything when sliding down the other side of the hill with the cemetery at the bottom.

Many are not maturing spiritually because they have never allowed faith to be a definite part of their lives. Yes, they would be insulted if their faith was questioned, but their giving depends on their bank account. If the bank account will not suffer, the check is written, but if it hits what they consider the low mark, they would not think of making a faith pledge if the money is not there. But Godly faith says, my God will supply that which I do not have in order to be faithful to what I've pledged. Most people's faith goes as far as they can see, never beyond what they can't see. But I charge, is that faith? Not according to the message our Lord preached on the Mount. Faith is stepping out into the unknown without anything, believing the living God will supply every need. Only that kind of faith will produce continuous maturity that will bless both God and man. Faith is an experience that will never be known, if faith does not reach beyond the immediate, then a lesser faith will not find rest in the unknown.

Becoming mature is a constant development that germinates the menial tasks that little children enhance. As children increase in the attributes that are God given, so must the Sanctified soul expand. These are sprouts that are so tender that they need gentle understanding overseeing their growth. The precious Holy Spirit is the cultivator of the fragile and lowly of heart.

Too many are so caught up in the experience of holiness that they can't handle the valleys that suddenly appear. What they thought could not happen, happened. Abruptly the joy turns to despair, the cloud with the silver lining is quickly a thunder storm that has tornado potential. How could this replace that feeling of ecstasy, with the shocking realization they are not as good as they thought they were, and there is no way to escape life's realism.

But feelings can get in the way of maturing growth. The highs and the lows usually end up in disheartening depression Sanctification does not do away with feelings, but these are placed under the Holy Spirit's control. Trials have their threats but maturity allows you to recognize these bumps that jar and intimidate for what they are, but that make victory that much more precious. God delights in His child that is not overwhelmed by life's sudden valleys, which only opens new doors that allows His child to move closer to Him. Peter's Spiritual maturity had reached unused understanding when he lodged with Simon the tanner who was participating in a ceremonially unclean occupation that was naturally abhorrent to the Jew He not only went to his home "but tarried many days."

Isn't this what Jesus did when He ate with the publicans and sinners, or asked water from the Samaritan harlot? Jesus had already displayed the necessary courage to break through centuries of prejudice and ceremonial law. Now, Peter needed to step into the path of Spiritual maturity. SPIRITUAL MATURITY DOES NOT MEAN LIBERALIZING BIBLICAL CONVICTIONS. IT MEANS, WALKING IN THE LIGHT THE HOLY SPIRIT GIVES. Not some Bible sniping professor who wears a smirk every time the "Book" is mentioned. That is not Spiritual Light, but detestable spiritual ignorance.

The God-man was completely holy from inception, but the physical needs maturing, "the child grew and waxed strong in spirit, filled with wisdom, and the grace of God was upon Him." The scripture does not recognize standing still, everything is a movement of forward or backwards. Spiritual maturity is always forward, but only that which is holy, not diseased, grows to bring forth good fruit. If the fruit is not good, it is cut down and cast into the fire. Quantity can always increase, but perfection in quality cannot increase. Purity is always pure, and can never be any more than that, but purity's volume must always increase while enlargement will maintain its purity. Purity abounds more and more in capacity, always expanding to acquire additional grace from God's boundless source. The receiving of His abundance depends upon the Spiritual appetite of each one of His children. The origin of God's Grace is limitless.

The opportunity to claim whatever is necessary for greater love, more patience, extra humility, larger faith is right there for those who would dare to conquer the ultimate within the confines of man's limitations. We have not because we ask not. There is no finality to even our limitations if it will glorify our God.

Spiritual maturity is advancing in the fruits of the Spirit, this fullness continues always within the reach of the most humble sanctified life. The process has years involved, which includes the mastery of God's Word; the daily cultivation of the prayer life; the gradual understanding of the leading of the Holy Spirit; the setting up of proper conditions to induce the inner life's desire to attract God's deepest aspiration for the soul. Who would dare to measure life short of God's purpose?

Spiritual maturity can also mean shedding, such as, ungodly and prejudiced attitudes; improper expressions; unsightly actions; unwise activities; an unbecoming approach to the opposite sex; hasty conclusions; legalistic notions; unsanctified personal appearance. This baggage will hinder any growth if not dealt with when the Spirit reveals the need. Our God wants the best, therefore, He brings to light the offensive mannerisms; the exaggerations that spill over the boundaries of truth. When one of the boys we had would start to tell something, the rest of the boys would look out of the corner of their eyes at one another. Why, because he always went over the boundaries of truth and they knew his exaggerations.

Poor Peter, problems seemed to follow him. The Holy Spirit had to confront him about not eating what God had cleansed. In order to convince him, the Lord had to give him a vision, so he would understand what was considered to be uneatable through tradition, God had cleansed. It appears at times, I'm like Peter, the Lord keeps pulling out things I need to discard if I'm to keep growing Spiritually. In fact, He is ever reminding, that the very appearance of evil is to be rejected.

The Spirit searches the past life for those things which will hinder and drag down any attempt for Spiritual progress. After signing his home and other property over to his wife, because of his considerable debt; he felt that the only way to save his home and property, was to claim bankruptcy. The law of the land excused his debts, but when he wondered why he wasn't growing spiritually, a higher law kicked in, and his conscience began to refuse any effort to excuse the former debts. If he was to retain his sanctification and mature as a holy whole Christian, he must start to repay every dollar he formerly owed. This is spiritual Light that cannot be refused if the holy walk is to continue. Who knows how many have been wonderfully sanctified by saying, "yes," but when revelation is given in areas that need the smelly garbage removed, the answer is, "no," the cost is too great, and the downhill slide is on the way.

Stagnation dies in God's presence. The nasty brackish spiritual condition is anything but purity or holiness without which there is no progressive maturity. The very spirit of the sanctified life must vindicate active spiritual development. It is perfect love in demeanor and manners which takes on new growth daily.

This growth is not undefined, nor imponderable, nor without direction or purpose, but is clearly defined with a uniqueness that is distinctly Divine. This route is a mounting faith upon more faith, a Grace that continually engulfs more Grace, a step to glory and a leap to still more glory, resulting in a firmly established foundation that leads to God's glory. Its countless degrees of progression are measureless. Only the individual can diminish spiritual growth, our God never will.

There is a vast differences between a perfect character and perfect love. Perfect Love is possessed at the act of Sanctification, while character is never complete, always being pruned, developed, cultivated and enriched by daily discernment under the impact of the Holy Spirit. Because of Sanctifying Grace, character is brought under the flavor and style of that fashioning Grace, much as a sculptor molds and chisels the granite to his liking. It is certain life has its hard blows, but when in the Master's hands each has its purpose. Our God never allows one too many blows.

Our Lord has placed within every living soul a thirsting desire to be like Him. Since eternity is within us, this will never die. Therefore, nothing else can satisfy. God's man refuses to be imprisoned by his carnal limitations. Carnal man is like a life within the cocoon fighting to free itself, so it can fly. As long as carnal man allows himself to be trapped within himself, all the fighting, action and effort can never free him. There must be the miracle of eternal life in sanctifying grace that frees him and permits him to fly with the heavenly. Now he is free to roam, to taste the flavor of God's creation. Each flower has a delicateness all its own. The more he flies the stronger his Spiritual wings become, thus enabling him to cover greater territory. That is sanctified man reveling in God's ever enlarging horizons. The superabounding Grace exceeds all expectations, sweeping man to new circles of glory.

Do we dare to speak of the fullness of God? Oh yes, we must! It is not that we have forgotten what has been done, but for the first time there is vision of what is out there. It has caught our imagination and passion, so much so that our ambitions for anything else has lost it favor. Our attraction is the prized of high calling of Him who so loved that He gave so I could enter into this matchless Grace with full expectation that the ultimate is to stand in His presence and hear Him says, "well done thou good and faithful servant." Then, It will be worth it all.

Meanwhile, there is much more territory to conquer. There are endless possibilities that take charge to accomplish that ultimate crown. The fullness of the Spirit pushes for the exceedingly abundant richness that nourishes the soul. The depth of First Thessalonians 5:14-24, or the Sermon on the Mount has barely had their surface scratched. Since eternity is wrapped in each scripture, there is no end; no dimension; no lack of capacity; no limit; it is there for the human mind empowered by the in dwelling Spirit to plunge into its infinite depths with Almighty God's blessing.

This is not a one-day lunge and then to be placed in the some closet until a future desire arises. This is a daily, hourly, moment by moment labor of love that demands excellence. There is no resting on yesterday's growth. That is what is so exciting, every day the Holy Spirit pulls back the veil and reveals new stimulating Truth that arouses a greater thirst and craving for more of the concealed treasures. Thank God there is always more there, no matter how many times we drink from His well.

Our God will never put restraints on our hungering and thirsting after righteousness, only man can do that. Man's enlargement of soul is a major thrust of the scripture. Babes in Christ are carnal; to remain babes in Christ can only sow devastating influence in all circles. What comes out of the mouth of carnal babes spreads shame on God's plan for living a maturing Spirit filled life. Partial obedience, is no obedience. Our Lord didn't go halfway to the Cross.

There are those who would hopelessly cling to the error, there is a gradual cleansing of the depraved nature and this is what they would called maturing, but in every scriptural case dealing with Sanctification it is complete, full, without degrees, always an instantaneous purification of the old nature. Then, maturity is without the obstruction of inner carnality, and can start its growth without carnal hindrances.

Maturity is an enlargement of Spiritual capacity that gives newness to the day knowing we are wrapped in His loving arms. It is the consciousness of His presence while putting on your socks or at the devotional time; the awareness of His presence as He actively holds Satan and his legions at bay or being knowledgeable of His healing grace; being conscious your Temple (body) is continually filled with Himself; or cognizance of personal communion no matter where you are, He is there.

It is a must that personal maturity is activated each day, but there is the need to reach beyond private concern to developing sainthood in others. There are so few who understand their own salvation, let alone trying to materialize and foster a plan for someone else. The task demands Biblical knowledge, with a Biblical Theology that brings it all together in sound sense for daily living. God's plan is always workable and practical. Without grasping the basics, the progress will be two steps forward and one step backward. This takes an eager mind with a persistent diligent will that is firmly rooted in a soul that has no other purpose than to glorify God. Developing a maturing wholesome saint with this mind set will be a fruitful ministry that will blossom and flourish, thriving on the meat of God's precious Word. The ministering and fostering of a chastening grace must be as cherishing as a nursing mother and as adamant as a stern holy father.

There is no way that maturing capacity will not be enlarged when the Spirit filled believer has one spiritual victory after another. These victories will not come but by deep abiding surrender that imparts His person and attributes in the Spirit filled man. This devoted surrender can conquer the anxiety of the poor, and crush the self-centeredness of the rich; quiet the fear of the afflicted and repress the antagonism of the powerful; lighten the heart of the lonely and dissipate the energies of the arrogant; solidify hope when it appears there is no hope; help us to enjoy plenty, and to be thankful in want.

With each triumph, soul capacity increases and devotion deepens. The soul rises to a higher state with a new song, "bless the Lord, O my soul: and all that is within me, bless His holy name." (Ps. 103:1) Soul enlargement enables His child to more fully understand how His goodness and mercy has lifted him out of nothingness, and cradled him to His bosom. Such spiritual achievements multiply the enjoyment of His presence and infuse the heart to delight in the heavenly.

Without the basic ingredients of Bible study and prayer there can be little soul expansion. Prayer opens new doors, integrates fresh and vital goals for spiritual improvement; unshackles the past; visualizes the future from God's prospective and encourages the present. Prayer enlightens the mind; energizes the will; fans the spiritual fires within; dispels spiritual ignorance; brightens the darkest path; releases Divine energy; and defeats the plans of the enemy. Prayer inspires maximum devotion and imitates the Master's example. Prayer is the soul's refuge, a shelter when violent storms threaten to sweep away faith's very foundation.

This maturity is not without spiritual conflicts. The powers of darkness will never cease their attack. But there will never be a time when our Lord is not in the midst of the battle. The Apostle Paul gives the completely surrendered Spirit-filled Christian's approach to this daily battle in these words: "Who shall separate us from the Love of Christ? Shall tribulation, or distress, or persecution, or famine, or nakedness, or peril, or sword? Nay, in all these things we are more than conquerors through Him that loved us. For I am persuaded, that neither death, nor life, nor angels, (fallen angels, or devils), nor principalities, nor powers" (no combination of devils or men), "nor things present, nor things to come, nor height" (of prosperity), "nor depth" (of adversity), "nor any other creature, shall be able to separate us from the love of God, which is in Christ Jesus our Lord." (Rom. 8: 35-39)

God's warrior does not shun or discount the seriousness of the conflict, but knows whom he has believed. Ultimate defeat is impossible. He lives or dies in utter confidence that physical life is not the end. His goal is to please the Father. "For our light affliction, which is but for a moment, worketh for us a far more exceeding and eternal weight of glory; while we look not at the things which are seen." (2 Cor. 4:17-18). The Apostle brings together Divine certainty, that this war that is raging is not ours alone, but has the overshadowing powers of heaven as agents of reinforcement that allows us to rest in their protective care. "Fear thou not, for I am with thee: yea, I will help thee; yea, I will uphold thee with the right hand of my righteousness." (Isa. 41:10)

Maturing is not necessarily a few enormous victories, but daily routine combative situations that are everyday conditions that can create a climate that wears on nerves. When conquest is achieved in this common arena consistently, the foundation has been built for the vicious attack that is sure to come later. It is settling into righteous living that has no appetite for the gratification of carnal enticing participation. The daily storms are the preparation for the tornado.

The maturing soul must understand the necessity of personal discipline, which is at the heart of building holy character. It is bringing a discipline will, to will God's will only. An undisciplined will can not be brought to the place of utter surrender to God's will. The will guides the whole being. But the will has a motivator in the nature, so it wills only what the nature is. A lady said she left her religion out of everyday life. That was all she had, just a religion like the heathen, but no living Christ. She willed to do what was convenient at the time, with no will to be continually mastered by the Master. Her arrogance revealed a person controlled by a will that was buried in a carnal nature that refused a discipline that would not yield any thing beyond herself.

Hopefully, it is understood maturity is not advocating a discipline swallowed up in legalism, or a cult, living a life like a mechanical drill sergeant. It is being God saturated, engulfed by the Holy Spirit, a willing love slave whose energies are freely given by a will that lost its will to God's will. Our God puts a needed governor on an uncontrollable life. When we are self controlled, we are out of control. Our boys only wanted to exert self will and would vehemently protect that right, even at the cost of lawlessness. But when brought under control, there was a relaxing, someone else was protecting and caring for them. Discipline did it.

A horse when hitched to the plow for the first time, kicks, tries to run, twists and turns, but when brought under control finds the plow a part of the day's work. Working with others is so much easier than running ahead, pulling the plow alone. When he pulls his rightful share, there is a relaxing that becomes restful. So it is with mankind. Self-will is very inadequate, it destroys inner rest. It is an upheaval, where there is no peace. Rest and peace go together, separate one and you do not have the other.

Discipline brings obedience, obedience brings surrender, and surrender brings His control. Israel never occupied Canaan just by entering it. Their victories came when they surrendered to God's leadership. This conquest did not come without considerable effort on their part. Confidence comes by the assurance that our God cares for His own. That is rest in the midst of violent turbulence, like the oceans whose waves are so high it appears they are trying to reach the heavens, and yet one half mile down, all is calm. Ah, sweet rest in the center of His will. Once this is experienced, it opens maturity's flood gates. The next battle gives more certainty, regardless of the circumstances, that disciplined obedience will bring another victory.

Everything about maturity centers around obedience that is disciplined. Prayer has little expectation if its motive is not wholly sealed in a disciplined obedience. Maturity demands that the hidden areas of life be uncovered, and known for what they are. There are multitudes who desire to be holy, filled with genuine joy, useful and who want to gain heaven, but who have not found that obedience is at the heart of all that is hoped for. The Apostle said it this way: "Hereby we do know that we are knowing Him if we are obeying His commandments. He that saith I know Him and obeys not His commandments is a liar and the truth is not in him." There is no possible way anyone can mature unless these conditions are met.

The great Welch revival resulted when church members who were professing Christians began to clear out their spiritual closets by confessing their lukewarmness, and known wrongs that needed to be made right to those who had been wronged. This fired the unsaved communities for miles around, 80,000 to 100,000 came to the understanding of obedience. Evan Roberts, who was at the center of this outpouring, said the message was: "Obedience! Obedience! Obedience!" Maturity rests squarely on obedience.

Maturity must face one test after another. A daring Faith is essential if these tests are going to experience victory. An obedient disciplined faith that is not resting on feelings is the fortress that will hold the soul steady when all sight is gone and the unseen enemy is attacking. It is the anchor that will not allow the soul to drift. There are certain trials that can arouse anxiety by their sudden appearance, and even shake faith for the moment, but then obedience claims audience, assuring that the moment is not all of life, and God is still God. Then rest steps in, and establishes the balance needed, remembering the embattled soul that has always found refuge under His wings. New faith has gained additional comprehension of the substance of things hoped for and the evidences of things not seen. With this outpouring of Grace comes a deeper expectation from the indwelling of the Holy Spirit. Once again the soul is set Godward.

Maturing Faith is expanded when it is tested. Faith is the root that takes a firmer hold on the pure nature, producing delicious fruit on which hungry souls can feast. Maturing Faith is not some kind of magic or exterminator that is to be used for personal gratification. It is the maintaining factor that is Divinely given for the personal communication with the Father. Is not that relationship holy? Then, in what areas is Faith to fulfill? Is not Faith's intent to deal with those issues that have an impact on the eternal soul? Holy Faith reaches Heaven but will not climb over known sin to get there. Faith may be hindered in its relationship to individual's physical and intellectual infirmities and the type of temptation (which is a way we can learn of our weaknesses), but these are only obstacles that give an added challenge to Faith's adequacy. Each test furnishes more evidence of Faith's qualification to be more than a match for any circumstance satan can place on our doorstep.

Maturing Spiritually is a refining process. A few ladies met together in Dublin to study the scriptures. While reading Malachi 3:3 they were struck by these words: "Shall sit as a refiner." One volunteered to call on a silversmith and see if the meaning could be clarified. The good man was more than willing to explain the refining process. Then the lady asked: "Sir, do you sit while the work of refining is going on?" "Oh, yes madam," he replied. "I must sit with my eye steadily fixed on the surface; for, if the time necessary for refining be exceeded in the slightest degree, the silver is sure to be injured." He had given her a picture of the scriptural meaning: "He shall sit as a refiner and purifier of silver." As the lady was leaving the shop, the silversmith called and said that he only knew when the process of purifying was complete, by seeing his own image reflected on the face of the silver's surface.

The Sanctified maturing soul will experience the refining fire that is not designed to destroy, but to purify to the extent that others can see the master reflected in you and me. Others are carefully watching to see if we produce damaged goods. Soul refining would never happen without the fire that heats the pot. This maturing does not happen in a moment's time, for daily new light will appear that will clear up yesterday's hidden mysteries. When we are walking on a misty morning and see an object at a distance, our knowledge of what it could be is imperfect. The object is not clear, so that it may be understood, because murky, unclear conditions exist, and no matter how hard we try there cannot be an accurate decision as to what it is. There is something there, but whether a human being or a gatepost, it too obscure to tell. After more distance is covered, it is a human being, but is he or she young or old, the thick haze makes it uncertain. Time brings us to complete comprehension of the person. But we went from a clouded indefinite knowledge to a correct understanding of what we first saw. If we keep walking with Him even when we cannot see what is ahead; in the Father's own time He will pull back the veil and reveal what we did not know. What ever it is, it will be for our good, but even after knowing, we may not know just how it will be for our good. Maturing Faith stands in its certainty that somehow it will be used to glorify our God, and to further shape our lives to be like His.

Dr. Craig Newton preached his last sermon to his church and gave an illustration something like this: A wise man told some children, who were going to cross the desert by night, that they should pick up the objects that glowed in the light of the moon. As they journeyed, the children picked up a few of the shining objects, a handful each. They could have filled their pockets, but picked up only what they could hold, passing by many that were equally large and brilliant. By morning, they were well past the desert and were now traveling in a new land. When the sun rose, they looked at the objects they had gathered. They were holding emeralds, diamonds, and other precious stones! They were exceedingly glad. Then, they were sad. Happy to have the treasure they had gathered, but sad that they had not filled their pockets to bursting with these precious gems. They could not go back for more.

Maturity opens God given choices. The right choice can have enriching treasures. But the desolate places are not attractive, and all that is wanted is just to get through the unpleasantries, but in doing so, we miss many of God's precious gems that He had made available only in that area. Most are seeking for these choice treasures in pleasing and agreeable surroundings, but only finding a small handful.

What a tragedy to be approaching the "new land" without possessing the many riches God had placed in the out of the way places, that could have been retained. It is necessary to note, there is no way that we can go back. Now is the opportunity to glean those eternal riches, tomorrow may be too late.

CHAPTER XI

GLORIFICATION
The ultimate

The ultimate is at hand for all mankind. The picture the Apostle draws is astounding and arresting, and should capture the heart of every honest soul. Read again these stunning words: "And I saw a great white throne, and Him that sat on it, from whose face the earth and the heaven fled away; and there was found no place for them. And I saw the dead, small and great, stand before God; and the books were opened; and another book was opened, which is the book of life; and the dead were judged out of those things which were written in the books, according to their works. And the sea gave up the dead which were in it; and death and hell delivered up the dead which were in them; and they were judged every man according to their works. And death and hell were cast into the lake of fire. This is the second death. And whosoever was not found written in the book of life was cast into the lake of fire." (Rev. 20:11-15)

This life's journey has ended, now another life is starting, standing in the presence of God, which for the redeemed, will be with Him forever. This is the "Blood Washed" last step, which is the "promised land." "Oh, that will be glory for me, glory for me, when by His Grace I shall look on His face, that will be glory for me." Then we can burst into the song: "Glorious freedom! Wonderful freedom, no more in chains of sin I repine! Jesus, the glorious Emancipator! now and forever He shall be mine." The faithful weary pilgrim has reached home.

Now standing in God's presence before the great white throne, all I have between me and hell is the covering of His Blood that washed my sins away, and my life lived in conscientious obedience. The awesome spectacle can bring terror or restful assurance. In the past life, I made a choice of who would be first in my life, and now that choice stands sealed, and will be mine for all eternity.

How sobering! For there are multitudes whose indifference and neglect have considered their personal goals were the first and the only necessary priority. Most thought a personal, "born again" experience was a relic of the past that has been buried in the advancement of the age. Their decision is cemented with them for all eternity. Take time to look into their eyes filled with reality's terror; see the agony in their face; hear the panic in their voice as the book opens to their account, and they know that it is not God's judgment, but rather their record that is their judge. God being Just, must carry out their decision. The opportunity has been locked into physical life's last breath. Now each will live with what has been a personal choice. If there is any blame, it rests on each individual's doorstep. All are without excuse. This judgment scene happens before our God makes a "new heaven and new earth."

Why? Because everything must fit into the framework of God's holiness, mercy, justice, love and righteousness. Therefore, the first Book opened revealed every detail of what the Trinity has done in order to save every lost soul. The utmost apex was Calvary, where God literally poured Himself out, emptying Himself for lost mankind. A price our imagination cannot comprehend. But this Book will also reveal the tears, the prayers, the heartache of those who prayed for your salvation. Everything Divinely possible was done to bring the need of Christ to personal attention. The accident, the sickness, the loved one snatched from your bosom, all were attempts the arouse the soul to the awareness that there was coming a day before the great white throne.

Of course, memory will be awakened as it was in the case of the rich man in hell who remembered. He could not forget his lifetime. Every minute detail that life gave will be burnt in the mind that is desperately trying to ignore the reality. There is no place to go to get away from the past life. It will be an endless movie. With all of the past raging through memory while standing at the Judgment bar; but already knowing personal accountability will demand punishment. The Lord will not need to say one word, past Christ rejection says it all. Guilt is like a raging inferno. That conscience that was hardened by years of resisting will burn like Herod's when He heard of the things Jesus was doing by saying, "this is

John the Baptist raised from the dead." The conscience he thought was dead, was resurrected.

The trial will not be long for there is not one single question asked, all motives are revealed, nothing can be hidden. All that can be done, is to look and see if your name is recorded in the Book of Life. The blazing presence of holiness and righteousness which will outshine the star, will quiet any attempt to explain why your name isn't there. Who would dare to question complete and holy purity which is above reproach?

There is no place in heaven for the unbelief of a half-hearted religion that has not completely changed the life from darkness to light. The greatest tragedy of all will be those who will hear the words: "Depart ye worker of iniquity, I know ye not."

Judgment is the first stage. The second stage is the "new heaven and the new earth." Our God must remove those things which are shaken. He speaks of a kingdom that cannot be shaken: "Yet once more will I make to tremble not the earth only but also the heaven."

The present earth must come to an end because of the gigantic upheaval caused when man sinned. The catastrophic event resulted in such violence that its tragedy is beyond repair. Sin's devastation has aroused such havoc there is no way God can remedy its rupture, but by making it new. The new earth will not contain any iniquity. It will be the paradise God envisioned when He first created it. In this new heaven and earth there will be perfect communion between redeemed man and His God, dwelling among His redeemed, diffusing His light and life everywhere.

Death will be destroyed after the general resurrection, for only the resurrection can destroy death. What was intended is now completed. The imperfections of humanity transformed into perfection, where the ideal will actually exist in the new Jerusalem.

The radiance of the heavenly city manifests only pure holiness, a garden of absolute paradise, where nothing can tarnish. The city's measures are that of a perfect cube, as was the Holy of Holies. Those who inhabit that city will continually be in the Holy of Holies, in which only the Priest could enter, but since each soul is their own priest through Christ, (the priesthood of all believers) all the residents are so privileged.

There the Presence of our God is, which will be a full communion never known before, no Temple is needed, because worship shall never cease. He is the Light where all things will be seen as they are. History has always been one of cycles, plunging from brilliance to darkness, but not so in God's city, constancy will continually abide. The mind will be so saturated by God's presence that for the mind to think anything else would be inconceivable. Jesus said there would be no giving or receiving marriage in Heaven. The intimacy of earthly relationships will not be condoned. There is nothing hidden or disguised, a completely different society. Continuing an earthly relationship, like with my dear wife, will not be. Will there not be a brother and sister relationship, taking on heavenly ties? Male and female will not have the earthly attractions. The fellowship of Believers will consume the feelings and emotions. God's presence will be the heart's desires. There will not be any room for anything else.

Who can dare to describe the beauty of true Holiness? Absolute purity, no trash dumps, nothing that defiles, every look is holy, every imagination sacred, every sound without discord, every musical note filled with harmonious virtue, every word framed in Truth, every transaction made in perfect honesty, every word spoken breathes holiness. Holiness' beauty shines and our gaze will never weary of its sight, everything done is an act of worship to our holy God. The soul will be fired with indescribable yearning to experience and learn more of Divinity's fullness. Pure gold is emblematic of Divine Nature, giving all their sense of worth. The saints will be permitted to eat from the tree of life, which will have 12 different fruits on it, bearing a different fruit each month. This is the tree that Adam and Eve were forbidden to eat of its fruits. No worms will be found in the fruit, no blight, nothing will be decomposed. All street cleaners will be relieved of their jobs.

Think of it, no disease, no sorrow, no tears, no crying, no pain, no death, no funerals, no parting, no nasty labels, no fear, no time clocks, for time will be no more, no street urchins, no homeless or lonely people, no hypocrisy, no lying, no fornicators, no temptations, no manipulative fraud, no crimes or murders, a land free of all and every sin conceivable. We long for peace and no more wars, our God has that place waiting for His faithful people. Its beauty is matchless as holy characters shine as lights walking those golden streets with voices at full volume singing ceaseless praises that will reverberate the heavens. Who would want to miss that

God-prepared place with its untold blessings? To miss heaven is the height of folly. Paul said this way: "...eye hath not seen, nor ear heard, neither have entered into the heart of man, the things which God hath prepared for them that love Him." (1 Cor. 2:9) Stretch your imagination as far as you possibly can and it will give only a small beginning of what awaits God's redeemed.

To the redeemed remember, God did not die for the fallen angels, but for fallen lost mankind. What a price He paid for our redemption! Friend this is our last step, hopefully, it will be into heaven's glory and not hell's fire. The thought humbles and crushes my heart as my time is quickly ebbing away. I shall live forever with the choice made at an altar of prayer. That day when I met Christ as my Savior becomes more precious by the moment. By His Grace I shall soon step on that Heavenly shore.